Not Afraid to Fall

Brian Hall

Printing and distribution:

BookBaby

7905 N Crescent Blvd,

Pennsauken Township, NJ 08110

Printed in the United States of America.

Editors: Chris Elliott & Cindy Beatty

Final Edit: Brian Hall & AutoCrit

Cover design, layout & artwork: Brian Hall

Photography credit: Richard Luff (back cover)

ISBN: 978-1-7342073-0-9

Website: https://notafraidtofall.com

Email: notafraidtofall@gmail.com

~ Marshall Moore ~

You're a true warrior my friend and a source of great inspiration to all who know you.

I am blessed by your friendship.

Dedication

This book is dedicated to my mother, Ruth, brother, Mark, and late father, Peter.

I would also like to dedicate this work to all people afflicted with Parkinson's disease, including their family and friends, for it is our family and friends who have to endure the worry of our affliction. Through their love, support, acceptance, and care-giving, we as Parkinson's patients have the opportunity to find a more self-accepting, productive way of life.

Foreword

I am delighted to have been asked by the author, Brian Hall, to write a foreword to his book. As a clinical neurologist, retired for the past thirteen years, this has given me an opportunity to catch up on Brian's illness, progress, and accomplishments since my retirement. His accomplishments especially have been impressive.

Parkinson's disease (PD) is one of the most common neurological disorders affecting approximately 1 percent of individuals over the age of 60. It is a progressive disability that cannot be halted but can be slowed by medical treatment and, as the reader of this book will learn, also by the patient's hard work, persistence, and guts. Chronic PD is primarily a clinical diagnosis based on the classic symptoms of a resting tremor, bradykinesia (slowness of movements), rigidity of the muscles (stiffness of muscles), and later in the course, declining postural stability (balance problems). The age of onset is usually between 40 and 70. The onset is rare before the age of 30. Those few cases with an early onset of Parkinson's disease (juvenile PD) often present with dystonias or the involuntary cramping of the muscles of the legs and lower arms. The more classic symptoms of PD appear somewhat later in the course of the disease.

Brian and his brother, Mark, experienced the onset of their illness in their early 20s with very painful involuntary twisting movements (dystonias) of their legs. The diagnosis of classic PD or juvenile PD was considered less likely partly because of the early age of onset, the obvious genetic factors (their father developed symptoms of Parkinson's disease much later in life), and their initial exquisite response of the painful dystonias to the drug dopamine (Sinemet). These facts suggested a related group of illnesses called Dopamine-Responsive-Dystonia (DRD). In DRD, painful dystonias normally precede the more classic symptoms of PD, which appear over the next several years. This variant of Parkinson's disease is characterized by a metabolic deficit in the brain cells responsible for the production of dopamine (a brain neurotransmitter). In Parkinson's disease, there is an actual loss of the brain cells producing dopamine. There have been more than two-hundred different genetic mutations described in DRD, but these defects only explain about 50 percent of all the cases of DRD. There is also a third group of diseases closely related to classic PD called Parkinson's plus diseases. These are not a consideration in Brian's case. The three variants of the disease are often generally referred to as Parkinsonism.

Without going further into boring medical details, we did look for a genetic dopamine deficit in Brian about fifteen to twenty years ago. But we came up empty-handed, as is to be expected. We also tried to boost these defective cellular pathways with certain co-enzymes and supplements, also without much success. Therefore, without a specific diagnosis possible at this time, Brian rightly will mention several of the possible diagnoses in the book and use them interchangeably. This is understandable and frequently done but can be confusing to the reader.

With this brief medical review (Brian will have much more to say about his illness,) we should turn our attention to Brian's very remarkable and special book. The first thing that attracts my attention is Brian's compelling description of his illness from a patient's point of view. This differs greatly from current fact-filled medical textbooks' dry characterizations. But if one reads the much older medical literature before there was as much known about various neurological illnesses, one can get a flavor of Brian's dramatic style of presenting his illness. He not only tells his story from the patient's side, letting us know all his unfortunate symptoms, but also how these symptoms are affecting him emotionally and his general well-being. Furthermore, Brian takes this a step further and tells us the results of our treatments, both the good, bad, and ugly.

Importantly, we learn how Brian reacts to his illness as it profoundly affects his life. We feel his struggles with the disease, his despair, his pain, his limitations, his resistance and his eventual acceptance of the challenge. But we also witness Brian rise to this challenge, learn to compromise with his disabilities, and fight to gain as much control as possible. We observe Brian's search for ways, both orthodox and unorthodox, some successful and some less so, to push back and to continue as normal a life as possible. Brian once told me that Parkinson's disease is "now a part of me and who I am, therefore I must not hide but learn to accept and live with it." A brave and insightful philosophy. I wish I could bottle it and pass it on to others!

We feel his elation and joy as he wins one hard battle after another with his illness. He never loses his sense of self nor his sense of humor, never withdrawing or hiding, never giving up his dream. In the book, he makes the reader cheer for him to reach his next goal, but we never feel sorry or sad for him. We applaud him as he descends Mont Blanc on skis and root for him to crest Mt. Washington on his bike.

There is a lot I would like to say about this book, but Brian does a better job! I am strongly recommending this book to nurses, health care providers, medical students, and physicians at all levels. The book reminds us that medical illnesses and their treatments have many effects on patients well beyond our office, the hospital, and the doctor-patient relationship. While it can be difficult, if the medical professions do not take these effects into consideration, we cannot fully treat the whole patient. We would be doing less than we are able for our patients. Brian also reminds us that the patient, when able, should be an active participant in his or her medical care and decisions. It is the patient who knows best or will suffer the most from our medical decisions. Brian, as usual, says it best when he tells us that the illness has become part of him (the patient), so how can the patient not be part of these decisions?

Family and friends of patients with any chronic illnesses will also benefit from reading this book. We often tend to withdraw from those with illnesses that are difficult for us to comprehend and cannot relate. Brian shows us how important those family members and friends are in his struggles. Their ability to sympathize, understand, and assist are crucial to his or her battles to live a more satisfactory and productive life.

Finally, this book deserves to not only be read but to become a guide for those with any chronic illness, not just Parkinson's disease. It is not how Brian responds to his specific illness but that he does respond. Each patient will have their own specific problems to face. Brian shows that with grit, determination, and help from others rewards are obtainable. He encourages others to find their own compromise with their own illness and to struggle on!

I cannot end without a few personal comments about Brian. I followed him for many years early in his illness before I entered retirement. Brian (and his brother, Mark) were always upbeat despite a frustrating life-changing illness. After some of his visits, while he was still able, Brian would take his guitar on the wards of the hospital and play for some of my patients, lifting both their spirits and mine. Writer Albert Hubbard said it best in a 1915 obituary for a dwarf actor, Marshall Pinckney Wilder, entitled "The King of Jesters," when he coined the phrase "He picked up the lemons that fate had sent him and started a lemonade stand.[1]" With his upbeat style, keen sense of humor (seen throughout this book), and his obvious desire to pass along the wisdom he acquired in his battles, Brian has made and drunk a lot of lemonade. He has made a profound impression on all he has met. I can just picture now, Brian chugging up Mt. Washington with a full glass of lemonade in one hand and a determined look on his face. The following poem by C.F. Flynn is my favorite variation of Hubbard's words and more appropriate here:

> "Life handed him a lemon,
> As life sometimes will do.
> His friends looked on in pity,
> Assuming he was through.
> They came upon him later,
> Reclining in the shade.
> In calm contentment, drinking
> A glass of lemonade.[2]"

1. Hubbard, Elbert (1922). <u>Selected Writings of Elbert Hubbard</u>. Wm. H. Wise & Co./The Roycrofters. Pp237. Archived from the original on September 8, 2012.

2. Flynn, Clarence Edwin (November 1940), <u>The Rotarian</u>, The Rotarian, p.62

P.S. A word to Brian: We always talked about an epic tennis match between us but as time passed your illness and my arthritic shoulder progressed! Brian, I know I would have beat the bejesus out of you, at least that is the way I want to remember it. I possibly could have. At least it would have been Titanic! Keep on trucking my friend. You are an inspiration to me and many, many others!

E. Prather Palmer, MD
February 2019

Preface

The physical and personal challenges I have had to face while on my journey with Parkinson's disease have taught me some of the most valuable lessons I have ever learned. These lessons have been universally beneficial to me and every facet of living my life. It is now my quest to share these lessons with Parkinson's patients and non-Parkinson's patients alike. Watching two other family members go through their own battle with Parkinson's, this disease has made a definite impact on me and my family. I have seen firsthand how no two PD afflictions are the same. I understand the unique and personal struggle each Parkinson's patient must undergo. Navigating through the treacherous waters of a diagnosis like Parkinson's, without question, can take the wind right out of your sails. I feel a strong commitment and obligation to share some of what I have learned from my situation, so as it might create a possible breeze of opportunity propelling you and your life forward. My goal and hope is to minimize the amount of time you might spend in mental anguish not over only Parkinson's, but any sort of mental, emotional, spiritual, and physical pain you may be experiencing in your life.

Acknowledgments

I would first like to thank Brenda Bliss. It was because of your initial encouragement, support, and idea I write this book. You always said I had something worthwhile to share with the world. Your encouragement, brought this book project from the shadows of my own mind to the tangible forefront of reality.

I would also like to express my deepest appreciation to my editor and dear friend, Chris Elliot. All along the way throughout this process, your help with this book project has been immeasurable.

From the age of 4 years old, Tim McLaren has been my best friend. Outside my family, no one knows my life journey with this disorder more completely or better than Tim. Tim witnessed the gradual progression of my disease, but his friendship never wavered. While I struggled to continue playing sports through my adolescent years, Tim was there. My early love of tennis somehow spilled over into Tim's life, and he and I shared many years of spirited tennis matches. When my foot cramps became an everyday occurrence, you graciously continued to play tennis with me, when nobody else would. Other people didn't understand or refused to wait for my cramps to subside. Tim, you always treated me as if I were never sick. What a gift! From the years before when I had no symptoms, you were there. Hockey games, skiing, school, and everything in between, we shared our youth. Now 53 years later, our friendship is stronger than it ever has been.

In addition, the consistent love and support of my friends such as Richard Luff, Peter Griffin, Frank Hyer, Michael Roy, Michele Westin, Jean Briggs and so many others. You ladies and gentlemen, and a great many of my other friends, accept me for the person I am. I have never felt you look upon me as a disabled person, but rather a person. It has been one the greatest gifts you could ever give me. Without question, your friendship and support I treasure perhaps more than you know.

Through the writing of this book, I have happily reconnected with my friend and former neurologist of more than fifteen years, Dr. Prather Palmer. In the early days of my journey with Parkinson's disease, his sound advice and wise words kept me safe from doing something that might make this challenging situation more catastrophic. The trust and immense respect you earned through my eyes as a patient, no other physician has ever duplicated. I am honored and incredibly grateful to have you write the forward of this book. Thank you, Dr. Palmer.

Bob Duffy, our ski trip to Europe in February 1992 was certainly a memorable one. Somehow you knew at that particular time in my life, a shared adventure would have an impact on me of epic proportions. It most definitely changed the direction of my life. You, could not have foreseen at the time skiing Mont Blanc would have such a profound effect on me, but it did! How do you thank someone for such a gift? The best I can do is to somehow pay it forward. Perhaps, in some of the pages of this book might be some needed inspiration for another person to incorporate into their lives? If so, I believe everyone who has invested in me, myself included, can feel a sense of peace and gratitude. Thanks, Bob.

My family has been a unique source of inspiration to me through the years. Mark, my brother, I want you to know I have learned much more from you than you ever have from me, probably in ways you don't even realize. Thank you for showing, and sharing your strength with me, Mark. Without you, I wouldn't know the acronym DBS.

Lastly, my mother, Ruth, is a shining example of the human spirit never giving up! The strength you have displayed during your own lifelong health battles did not go wasted on me. Rather, your strength became a playbook for me to go to during my own times of need. I would like to think we share that quality, mum. I love you.

Thank you, one and all.

If you want to move forward in your life,
I found it's best to look forward...

Brian Hall

Mount Washington Auto Road Bicycle Hillclimb.

August 2018

Introduction

These days I wake up happier and healthier then I have been at any other point in my life. Safe in the fact of knowing I have not beaten Parkinson's disease, I've made friends with it. Perhaps some of you are wondering what I mean. How do you make friends with a disease? I strove to accomplish this when I notice while fighting the disease, just how much I was actually fighting myself.

I wholeheartedly believe it's not diseases that cripple people, but rather the mental stigma of feeling less than you once were that really has a disabling effect on a person's life. When we buy into feeling we are less, we start doing less. And this is a slippery slope for anyone to try to navigate. In my particular case, I was consumed by my fears of feeling less, making it impossible to find a clear path toward self-acceptance.

The process of cooperating and adjusting to your situation in life is one of the great lessons Parkinson's disease has taught me. It has been the most comprehensive pain management course I could ever hope to enroll in. Through the years, the acceptance and patience I have had to learn while on this journey has helped to heal all aspects of my being. In many ways, Parkinson's saved me, and has truly introduced the real Brian, to me.

In January 2019, I turned 57, marking forty-three years of DRD/PD (Dopa Responsive Dystonia / Parkinson's Disease.) A milestone indeed. What makes my story compelling is not only the length of time I have been afflicted with the disease, but also how I have come to live in harmony with the disorder.

In October 2007, I underwent brain surgery to have bilateral implants for a DBS operation, (Deep Brain Stimulation) for the express purpose of abating my symptoms of Parkinson's disease. Ten months later in August 2008, I came to a decision to discontinue all the drugs and medication therapies I had been taking for Parkinson's disease. Most of this medication I had been taking for well over twenty years.

While my decision to stop my medication was not supported as a sound medical approach by my doctors, I am pleased to say for over eleven years I have been medication free. I feel so much better than I did while on a drug therapy program. How is this possible? I was open. Open for change and willing to try to take medical measures which only made sense to me. While my approach to living with Parkinson's is completely unorthodox in the face of all traditional methods, I've taken a turn toward a healthier path, as the disease goes merrily on.

When my personal pride made room for humility, then and only then did the possibility for change occur in my life. During my youth, I thought I was entitled. Entitled to live a life of good health. What I have learned is no one is entitled to anything in this world, especially good health. Health is a gift most of us abuse or take for granted until it's too late. When the hand of fate knocked me off my horse, I was, without a doubt, shocked. To this very day, I refuse to believe having PD or any other catastrophic disease can keep anyone out of life. If you wish to live, you simply climb back on your horse and keep on riding. Ralph Waldo Emerson wrote, "Health is the greatest wealth." This quote rings truest with the people who have been humbled by a disease or a chronic illness.

Whether or not you have good physical health, in my opinion, does not determine one's overall health picture. Being healthy can be as much a mental process as a physical challenge. But the responsibility for your own health is ultimately up to you. No doctor or medication in the world will be more in tune with you day in and day out than yourself. It is always good to remember to use the resources you have available to you wisely and to your advantage. In my case, time revealed to me just how much responsibility I gave away to doctors, medications, and anything else offering me a chance to be well. Only when I took some of the responsibility back for my own health did I feel empowered and on a healthier course. Empowerment came back to me when I returned to a routine of working out, eating healthier, and doing as much as I could do for myself.

Living with Parkinson's disease is not what you might think. After all this time, I have to say it has been both the best and worst thing that has ever happened to me.

This is my story of being lost as a young man and how having Parkinson's disease helped me to find myself. When you are lost, admitting that you are is the hardest part, and the first step to being found.

Disclaimer

One of the most interesting and unusual characteristics of Parkinson's disease is that no two patients' symptoms are identical. The means in which I have found my relief, as stated in this book, may or may not help or work the same for you. Over the years, it has been my experience that what works today to keep the symptoms of Parkinson's at bay, won't necessarily work tomorrow. As Parkinson's patients, we must remain ever vigilant to discover new ways to keep our own Parkinson's symptoms under control. It is my goal that sharing my story helps to motivate you to start or keep looking for the answers that you need, while on your own personal path with Parkinson's. I pray for your wellness and that you may find strength you never knew you had as you embark or continue on your journey with Parkinson's disease.

Chapter 1 - Out of Nowhere

I'm not what you would call a shy or meek person. Never have been. Quite the opposite, in fact. At a young age, I often sought out and found enjoyment exploring any and all physical challenges. In my earliest childhood recollections, I felt a definite physical connection between my body and my brain. This connection granted me abilities in numerous sports I loved participating in. In my head, I could picture what I wanted my body to do and did it. I also grew up with an acute sense of how things looked. More accurately, how I looked. What mattered to me early on in life was the world's perception of me. I doubt I was alone in feeling this way. I was not any different from all the other kids I grew up with. From childhood, I loved sports, music, and being outside. When I was a youngster, being inside was like a jail sentence! My, how things have changed.

Growing up in the seacoast part of New Hampshire, there are many reasons for a youngster to be engaged in outdoor activities. The Granite State is a wonderful place to be a kid. It has incredible beauty in every region. We have the Lakes region, the Atlantic Ocean, and the White Mountains, for outdoor playgrounds. Throughout my life, I have utilized them all - from skiing, to scuba diving, and almost everything in between. Being actively engaged as a child was as much a part of my life as breathing. The region of New Hampshire I am from is, forty-five minutes north of Boston and two to three hours from some fabulous skiing, perched right on the Atlantic Ocean. If you have never visited here, I would encourage you to make the trip. It's well worth it.

From the start, my personality and interests were divided - split between a love of music and a love of sports. At the age of 9, I took up a life-long passionate affair with the guitar and songwriting. This led me to music college. Even earlier in my childhood, I had a natural ability in basketball, hockey, skiing, and particularly tennis, which led me to teaching tennis. These early developmental years were joyous and carefree.

It was not until 1976 I started noticing physical issues in my lower extremities. It first presented itself to me as foot cramping. What I know now as "Dystonia."

("Dystonia is a neurological movement disorder syndrome in which sustained or repetitive muscle contractions result in twisting and repetitive movements or abnormal fixed postures.")
wikipedia.org https://en.wikipedia.org/wiki/Dystonia

Initially, these cramping events were sudden and intermittent, and the duration of these episodes was short. The pain was not too severe, but it was enough that I had to take notice, and was strange nevertheless. I participated in basketball and hockey teams all throughout junior high school, and this had not been an issue thus far. Frankly, I found the entire phenomenon, baffling, to say the least.

In 1976, it was our nation's bicentennial summer celebration. The summer seemed to fly by. Still, I was filled with the anticipation and excitement of starting my freshman year in high school at Winnacunnet High the coming fall. Being 14 years old, naive, immature, young and slightly overconfident I took on high school like most freshman do. Like a deer in the headlights of an oncoming vehicle. After the first few weeks of school and the normal pomp and circumstance were over, basketball tryouts were held. I desperately wanted to make the team. Many of the kids I had played with all throughout junior high school were there to try out too. In junior high, in the league I played in, I had earned the reputation for never quitting. Being one of the shortest players on the team, I would not shy away from getting down low in the paint, battling for rebounds. Stealing or picking the ball away from a taller opponent, without committing a foul. I was a quick player, with good eye-hand coordination. In addition to those skills, I was a competent outside shooter as well.

There were many students in the gymnasium, myself included, shooting around before the tryouts, basically warming up. All of a sudden, I heard a whistle blow. It was the coach. He wanted to give us our instructions and assignments. Coach Ford was a tall and somewhat intimidating character, and when he said move, you paid attention. It wasn't long into the tryouts when Coach Ford noticed I was having trouble moving up and down the court. He pulled me aside to ask me what was the matter. I explained to him recently I had been having an issue with foot cramps, and they would come and go without warning. Finishing up the tryouts with the coach's watchful eyes upon me, I knew now I was on his radar. Afterwards, he came up to me and said, "Brian, it's not your skills on the basketball court that's the issue here. It's your inability to draw on them at certain times that is a concern to me and this team." I did not make the Winnacunnet Warriors basketball team that year, but Coach Ford's concern would become my own soon enough. Disappointing, but not earth - shattering. I thought to myself, more time for the old paper route.

Tennis was another sport I really loved. Probably more than any other sport, tennis taught me the mental aspect of any physical challenge. I grasped this concept early on in life playing tennis. Tennis is very much like playing a physical chess match with your opponent. The best way to explain what I am talking about is the only difference between the number-one tennis player in the world and the number-two player is not how physically tough the player is, but rather how mentally gritty they play the game. The true nature of tennis has always appealed to me and my own nature.

I began playing tennis when I was a youngster, about 9 or 10 years old. Our junior high school did not have a tennis team, so I was excited to get to the high school level and show my stuff. The coming spring I was going to make the Winnacunnet Warriors tennis team. Leaving behind the embarrassment of my failed attempt to make the basketball team the previous fall, with fingers crossed, off I went.

The tryouts were informal. Coach Carrier started pairing us up, so he could watch our groundstrokes as we hit against each other. I was hitting against one of the other kids who was trying out for the team, when out of nowhere, I began having such painful foot cramps I could not even stand. The cramps knocked me flat. Sitting Indian style on the court clutching my feet, in agonizing pain. When the coach asked me what was wrong, I had no idea what to tell him. He asked, "Can you move?" I replied, with a resounding, "NO!" A few minutes went by, and I could feel everyone's attention on me as the tryouts were paused. Then the coach said to me, "If you can't get up, how can you possibly play a match and be a member of this team? Brian, I think you have to forfeit and forget about making the team this year." Hearing those words come from his mouth were extremely disappointing, but I told him that I understood. I tried to stand up, but no matter how hard I tried I could not make it to my feet. Shocked, I had to sit there until the pain subsided. I recall hearing a good friend of mine saying to some of the other kids at the tryouts, he thought I was faking it. Hearing this made me feel even worse. After a long rest, I finally made it to my feet and rode my bicycle back home. We lived in the general vicinity of the high school. Our house was maybe a mile away, and I used to ride my bike to and from the school all the time. I was having a hard time believing that anything could be seriously wrong. Being just as active as all the other kids were back then, none of this was making any sense. What the hell was going on with me?

This time period was around the same time my parents started to have difficulties in their marriage. There was a great deal of tension building between them. The problems and issues they were having had remained unresolved and dormant for years. This tension resulted in a divorce in 1976 after sixteen years of marriage. I was 14 at the time, and I took the news of my parents' breakup pretty hard. Outwardly, I put on a brave face and seemed fine. Inside I was trying to grapple with the reality of what this meant to my family and the details of all the changes heading my way. To top it off, we were going to have to move. My mom, brother, and I were all moving to Exeter, which happened to be the rival school district to the town of Hampton. In my opinion, this was not a favorable decision, but I did my best to take it all in stride. Though, the more I tried to ignore these impending changes, the more it got under my skin. I kept trying to tell myself life goes on as it does for everyone, and as it did for me and my family. However, this life-altering event was not going to change my life or slow me down. Or so I thought.

Exeter and Hampton are about seven miles apart geographically speaking, but in terms of the towns, they were worlds apart from each other. My interpretation back then was Hampton was this laid back, cool beach community, while Exeter, famous for Phillips Exeter

Academy, had this elitist vibe and felt a bit full of itself compared to Hampton. Phillips Exeter Academy is one of the most highly regarded private prep schools in the country. The most elite students from all over the world attend PEA. It is a breeding ground for the Ivy League, a mold I certainly was not suited for. However, attending Exeter High School felt much different from Hampton, and was.

In the summer of 1977, we successfully moved into a condominium in Exeter, New Hampshire, one town inland from Hampton. Our new digs at the condo had a pool and a couple of tennis courts, which was exciting. By the time we moved and got settled in, my mysterious medical condition had become much worse. The summer of '77 was my summer of change, going through puberty. I believe whatever was happening to me medically, when it collided with all the chemical changes puberty brings, it made my symptoms much more acute. The frequency and severity of the pain was increasing. Furthermore, the foot cramping was becoming more noticeable to me and to all who were around me. The pain was so excruciating it would stop me dead in my tracks. I had no other choice but to yield to it. Worse yet, the cramps were rogue. I could not predict how long they would last or when they were coming. It got to the point where I went out to play a tennis match for an hour and a half, and for half the match I would be on the ground trying to find some relief from those blasted foot cramps.

All of a sudden, being an Exeter Blue Hawk somehow depleted my interests in being involved in playing high school sports. Basketball season came and went that year with a yawn, as did the whole fall/winter sport season. However, there was still one winter sport I didn't have to choose sides to participate in, and I loved it as much as any other sport. It was skiing!

The Mount Washington Valley any time of the year is impressive, but in winter it is absolutely magnificent. Schussing down one of its frosty peaks and experiencing the freedom that only skiing can provide one's spirit wasn't just a passion back then. It was a full-blown childhood addiction. While on one of those snowy peaks during the winter of 1977 - 78, I caught a real serious glimpse of the trouble that was heading my way.

In North Conway, NH. I was 15 years old and skiing some familiar, easy terrain at a ski resort I had skied countless times. Skiing the fall line on the far left side of the trail, when out of nowhere I "lost it," ending up in the woods. I hit the frozen ground with a tremendous force. For no apparent reason, my legs stiffened, suddenly giving way, resulting in a fall that could have had catastrophic consequences. I did not sustain any sort of serious injury, but it did freak me out. I remember thinking to myself, "I should be improving as a skier, why am I falling like this?"

What made this particular fall so memorable was the way I fell – 100 percent out of balance, unable to control my legs. Going from being in complete control one moment, then completely out of control the next. I had never felt that feeling before on skis or otherwise in my young life. At the time, I laughed it off, and told my friends I caught an edge, hiding from my embarrassment. But I knew this was getting serious. After, I began to pay a bit more attention to my balance, and intermittently I could see even walking was beginning to become more of a problem. I learned quickly how to minimize attention and suspicion. Most people had no idea anything was wrong. And that was just the way I wanted it.

The more outward and apparent my symptoms were becoming, the more I would attempt to hide them and go inward. In no way did I want to be seen as different. No one does, do they?

My sophomore year at old Exeter High School, I was pretty much to myself, but, not friendless. Sadly, the year was turning out to be unquestionably lackluster, being the new kid in the rival school, dealing with a mystery physical ailment. I became so withdrawn during those years, more than any other time in my life. Somehow, I always had a good outlook about things though, as I struggled on with the foot cramping, keeping it to myself. What choice did I have?

In the grand scheme of things, my day-to-day life had not been affected all too much. It hadn't stopped me from being who I was. The momentary interruptions I covered up with excuses. What I was experiencing was only the tip of the iceberg. What lies beneath the surface for my future would be much more severe. Regardless, a pattern began to form through the pain. Whenever I would feel cramps coming on I would find a quiet place to hide, a bathroom, a closet, a dark empty room, whatever. I began isolating myself away from everyone, to be alone with the pain I was going through.

As I was walking the halls at Exeter High School in between classes, I passed by the guidance counselor's office along the way. Hanging on the wall outside the office they had a poster that was awe-inspiring. It was the image of a man strapped to a wheelchair climbing a vertical face of a cliff, hoisting himself up this massive rock ledge with only a rope. The caption read, "The only limitations we have, are the ones we place on ourselves." These words and image definitely affected my life. It showed me whatever any one of us faces, the human spirit can do amazing things. The imagery and symbolism of the poster live with me still to this very day.

Armed with a new hope and optimism in the spring of my sophomore year, I told myself I would try out for the Exeter tennis team. Carlo Nittoli, who was my world history teacher at the school, was also the tennis coach during the spring of 1978. Mr. Nittoli as a teacher had an easygoing style and attitude. His approach in the classroom was always warm and friendly.

Before the tennis tryouts, I wanted to be up front with Mr. Nittoli, so I told him what had happened in the past trying out for other tennis and basketball teams. He said, "Why don't we just see how you do?" reassuring me to come and try. The day of the tryouts arrived. I was on the court hitting against Mr. Nittoli with two other students, so it was doubles. I was at the baseline in the add court, and Mr. Nittoli was at the net in the opposing deuce court. More like right on the net! I asked him if he could back up a bit while we rallied. He smiled and said he was fine, not to worry! I always had an aggressive forehand and I knew if I caught it just right, Mr. Nittoli would be wishing he had a helmet on, or that he had backed up. Sure enough, I creased a forehand right at my coach. The ball ricocheted off his head with a reverberating THOP, "Half thud, half pop." Carlo went to the ground. Oh my god, I thought, I have injured the coach the first day out. I went to the net to see if he was all right, and just before I reached him my foot cramps violently appeared. I became almost rigid from the shins on down. The pain was unimaginable! I apologized to Mr. Nittoli for hitting him on the head with the tennis ball, but he was more concerned for me at that moment than himself. I had beaned this man harder than I had ever beaned anyone in my life. He simply got up, smiled, and turned his attention toward me, and the business of coaching the team.

For the rest of the tryouts I wrestled with myself in the corner, trying to relieve my foot cramps. Again, turning inward to deal with the pain. When I was able, I got up to go find a suitable place to hide. My pattern was coming into full bloom. Later on, Mr. Nittoli kindly let me know his obvious decision about me not making the tennis team.

Back then, I couldn't talk about it with anyone because the problem was so intermittent. I just had no idea what was going on with me at the time. More importantly. I was so embarrassed and frustrated with my situation. Quite literally I had no answers. Being the new kid living in Exeter wasn't helping my situation all that much either.

The school year drew to a close, making way for summer vacation. Summer 1978 was my first summer having a car and a driver's license. This made Hampton, the beaches, and my friends much more accessible. Some of my Hampton friends even came to the condo to play tennis. Things felt like they were getting better, with the newfound freedom of having a car and a license, but regardless it was a rough summer of tennis.

The foot cramping was getting more severe. It was happening more and more frequently and for longer periods of time. The cramps would manifest themselves in either foot or in both feet. My toes would curl down uncontrollably like a ballerina's or curl directly up backward, toward my head. Sometimes one foot, the toes would curl downward, while the other foot, the toes would curl backward. Whenever any sort of cramping occurred, I would have to walk on the sides of my feet. This made me susceptible to rolling an ankle and falling.

At the ripe old age of 16, I scheduled an appointment with a local neurologist. I remember thinking to myself, there has got to be a pill I can take for this? Right? The day of the appointment I wasn't too nervous, but I was all alone. I actually felt pretty good and relieved that maybe I would finally be getting some answers to this mystery. I took a seat in the waiting room at the Exeter Clinic and did what I could to organize my thoughts. "The doctor will see you now," a soft voice uttered from behind the glass window. I rose, entering his examination room. The doctor held out his hand to greet me and then asked, "What seems to be the trouble?" Doing my best, I explained all the events leading up to requesting the appointment with him, describing my symptoms clearly and concisely. I Expressed great concern for what was happening to me, and the seriousness of the pain. After being there a total of maybe twenty minutes, no tests, no real examination, just a Q & A session and I had my answer. He told me it was "Psychosomatic." Psychosowhat? When I asked the doctor what that really meant, I learned a huge lesson about people and about myself, and that was this. Never let the power of anyone's words - good or bad - define who you are or influence what you know to be true about yourself. The one thing I did know was it wasn't psychosomatic!

So not knowing what to do next, I did nothing. I continued being the active kid I always had been. Stoically ignoring the pain and doing the activities regardless. If I ignored the pain and didn't allow people to see me hurting, I thought that it would go away. This could not have been further from the truth! The more I refused the pain as a part of me, the further away from myself I became. In the beginning, I really thought I was fighting the good fight against whatever physical demon was inside me. The fact was I had waged an internal war against myself, refusing to accept who I was or what I was going through. This knowledge I eventually came to embrace took years to realize and most of my life to comprehend.

The answers I was hoping to get from a neurologist could have helped me in those early years to stop hiding. Rather than helping me and my situation, it solidified the pattern of hiding from the pain and refusing to share it with anyone. At the time, I was doing my best with the cards life had dealt me. But how could I answer anyone's questions about my health condition when I didn't know myself. I opted to avoid the whole mess and preferred not to talk about it. Anyway, it was all in my head, right?

Chapter 2 - Cramping My Style

Condominium living and its tightly structured way of life did not fit anyone's independent nature in my family. My mom, brother, and I didn't conform well to the rigidity of our new living environment. Rules, associations, and committees were all a necessary evil to making that sort of living situation work, I suppose. We could see straight away it wasn't for us.

With my junior year coming to a close and my brother soon to be graduating from Exeter High School, my mom made arrangements to move back to Hampton in the spring of 1979. She bought a modest cape, in a quiet, rural neighborhood. All I knew and cared about was, I was going home. This enabled me to finish my senior year of high school back in Hampton, which, pleased me greatly! Those two years spent in Exeter were indeed a brief moment in time. Though, it is etched in my mind as the point where everything in my life went sideways. During the haze of the initial move, losing my dad, coupled with trying to fit in at a rival school, it was a complete fiasco. Not to mention my attempts to adjust to an undiagnosed medical issue. All of this really affected my psyche in ways I could not see at the time.

For the next few years, I struggled with the mysterious foot cramps. As time went on, the cramping got worse and started to weave its way into every facet of my life. My foot cramping was advancing from being solely brought on by sports to being brought on by walking and standing as well.

The one and only activity I had to console me was music. I played the guitar and continued my interests in songwriting all throughout junior high and high school. Music had always spoken to me through difficult times when nothing else did or even could. Whether it was foot cramps, my parents' divorce, or anything at all started to derail me, music always put me back on the right track again. Writers like John Lennon, Paul McCartney, George Harrison, David Gates, and Jim Croce wrote inspirational songs. These songs and what the music made me feel when I listened to these artists helped me to realize I wasn't alone in this world. I then saw everyone has their own problems to come to terms with. Being a part of this world means figuring out how you fit in it. Music was a vehicle that I used to find my way. These amazing writers and others touched my life in such a profound manner I feel indebted to them even still. Music became a sanctuary and the vehicle I used to move my life safely forward.

Around 1983, the pain and frequency of the foot cramping became intolerable. Once again, I sought help from medical professionals. This time, I wasn't fooling around with local doctors. I needed the best. So I contacted the neurological department at the Lahey Clinic, in Burlington, Massachusetts to set up an appointment. I was referred to a Dr. Palmer, a senior neurologist on staff at the time. Right away I liked him and felt comfortable with his approach to my medical situation. Dr. Palmer was unlike any other physician I had ever met. He seemed genuinely concerned for my well-being and interested in the medical challenges that my mysterious case posed. He wasted no time trying to figure out the cause of the foot cramping. Tests, tests, and more tests. Days turned into weeks, weeks turned into months, months turned into years. It all came back the same, negative. Dr. Palmer announced, "Brian, you're the healthiest sick person I have ever met!" I thought to myself, well that's nice. After years of countless blood tests, evoked response tests, spinal taps, MRIs, including cutting-edge nuclear photon scans, I was hoping for a bit more information than this. Dr. Palmer had a much more difficult time telling me that he knew nothing than I did hearing him admit it. Though, I could tell just how much it upset him, being unable to provide me with a diagnosis. How invested he was to help me. He had become much more than my doctor. He had grown into a caring friend and health ally. Regardless, I was beginning to see the toughest part about being a patient was learning to be patient.

Remaining positive, I kept thinking to myself, if all of these tests are coming back negative, maybe the problem is nothing to worry about. At this moment, I found solace in not knowing, which made no sense at all. Countless tests, over many, many years, with no answer to my medical problem. I was stalemated because Dr. Palmer had run out of tests to give me, except for one. It was an arterial graft of the spine. He had noticed something on one of my MRIs, and thought it might be worth exploring. This test came with very high risks, and could leave me paralyzed. Furthermore, there was a low chance they could do anything to remedy a problem, if they could even identify a problem existed. This didn't strike me as a very good option. As eager and hopeful as I was for a solution to my cramping, this procedure was far too intrusive and risky to even consider. Dr. Palmer agreed with me. I kept seeing him for medical checkups about once every other month. He would examine me to see if the disorder was progressing, which it incrementally was. Also, he would update me with anything new that might offer some help to my situation. These sorts of appointments went on for some time, I believe years. Until, remarkably he had something for me that he said he felt hopeful about. Puzzled and excited, I asked him what it was. He said it was a drug called Sinemet, used for Parkinson's patients who were deficient in dopamine. Dr. Palmer also said whether it helped or not either way we would learn something valuable. Skeptical, I took the prescription he wrote and did not fill it for six months. I needed to read as much as I could on the drug. I wanted to be sure of the possible side effects and its safety. This was a few years before the internet, and researching topics such as this was not as easy as it is today.

Sinemet - ("Carbidopa/levodopa, also known as levocarb and co-careldopa, is the combination of the two medications carbidopa and levodopa.[1] It is primarily used to manage the symptoms of Parkinson's disease but does not change the course of the disease.[1] It is taken by mouth.[1] It can take two to three weeks of treatment before benefits are seen.[2] Each dose then begins working in about ten minutes with a duration of effect of about five hours.[2][3] Common side effects include movement problems and nausea.[1] More serious side effects include depression, low blood pressure with standing, sudden onset of sleepiness, psychosis, and increased risk taking behavior.[1][4] Carbidopa prevents the breakdown of levodopa outside the brain.[4] In the brain, levodopa is broken down into dopamine by which it has its effects.")

After mulling it over a long while, reading about the side effects on as much information as I could find, it didn't seem to be too harmful. So I figured it was worth a try. I called Dr. Palmer, to let him know I would be filling the prescription after all, and off I went to the pharmacy.

This medication was far from cheap. In fact, it was extremely expensive! I believe the original script as written was 25/100 mg, three times a day. If my memory serves me correctly, a month's supply of sinemet back then ran in the hundreds of dollars, between $750 and $850, more or less.

(The history of levodopa, beginning with its isolation in 1910-13 from seedlings of Vicia faba to the demonstration, in 1961, of its "miraculous" effect in patients with Parkinson's disease (PD). Midway between these two time points, in 1938, L: -dopa decarboxylase was discovered, the enzyme that produces dopamine (DA) from levodopa. In 1957, DA was shown to occur in the brain, and in 1959 it was found to be enriched in the basal ganglia. At that time the striatal localization of DA, together with studies done in 1957-58 in naive and reserpine-treated animals regarding DA in the brain and the central effects of levodopa, suggested its possible involvement in "extrapyramidal control" and "reserpine parkinsonism". Following these discoveries, a study of (postmortem) brains of patients with basal ganglia disorders, including PD, was started, demonstrating, in 1960, a severe striatal DA deficit specifically in PD, thus furnishing a rational basis for the concept of "DA replacement therapy" with levodopa. Accordingly, in 1961, the first highly successful clinical trial with i.v. levodopa was carried out. In 1963, the DA deficit in the PD substantia nigra was found, indicative of a nigrostriatal DA pathway in the human brain, subsequently established in animal studies in 1964-65. In 1967, the

chronic, high dose oral levodopa regimen was introduced in treatment of PD. Besides the above highlights in the history of levodopa, the article also cites critical opinions of world authorities in brain research of the time, harmful to the cause of DA, levodopa and PD. Today, the concept of DA replacement with levodopa is uncontested, with levodopa being the "gold standard" of modern drug treatment of PD.) pubmed.gov https://www.ncbi.nlm.nih.gov/pubmed/21080185

My first two weeks on the drug Sinemet, I really didn't see any changes in my condition or feel any different. I was still experiencing extreme pain from foot cramps and like always they would appear out of nowhere. When the third and fourth week came, it was as if god himself suddenly made my symptoms and painful cramps go away. It was nothing short of a miracle! It was around 1987-88, and I could not wait to share the life-changing news with Dr. Palmer. He had worked so hard and never given up on me. This was a triumph for the both of us to share. Upon feeling better, I immediately drove to Lahey Clinic to see the doctor without an appointment. I walked briskly and confidently up to the reception desk on the neurological floor. I stated I didn't have an appointment, but I needed to see Dr. Palmer right away. The receptionist said, "Take a seat." Waiting in the neurological department with an enormous smile on my face, I could hardly contain the joy I was feeling during this moment. When Dr. Palmer saw me, he knew. He knew he had somehow helped me to lift the weight of the world off my shoulders. As I stood up, to greet the man who freed me, I could see in his eyes he felt as good as I did about it. I asked if this meant we knew what this was. He smiled and said it looked like dopa responsive dystonia. Finally, after all this time, something to call this nightmare. Dr. Palmer said, "I want to see you in two weeks," and we made another appointment. I felt right then I had a new beginning and I wasn't going to waste a second of it.

("Dopa-responsive dystonia") is a disorder that involves involuntary muscle contractions, tremors, and other uncontrolled movements (dystonia). The features of this condition range from mild to severe. This form of dystonia is called dopa-responsive dystonia because the signs and symptoms typically improve with sustained use of a medication known as L-Dopa.

Signs and symptoms of dopa-responsive dystonia usually appear during childhood, most commonly around age 6. The first signs of the condition are typically the development of inward- and upward-turning feet (clubfeet) and dystonia in the lower limbs. The dystonia spreads to the upper limbs over time; beginning in adolescence, the whole body is typically involved. Affected individuals may have unusual limb positioning and a lack of coordination when walking or running. Some people with this condition have sleep problems or episodes of depression more frequently than would normally be expected.

Over time, affected individuals often develop a group of movement abnormalities called parkinsonism. These abnormalities include unusually slow movement (bradykinesia), muscle rigidity, tremors, and an inability to hold the body upright and balanced (postural instability). The movement difficulties associated with dopa-responsive dystonia usually worsen with age but stabilize around age 30. A characteristic feature of dopa-responsive dystonia is worsening of movement problems later in the day and an improvement of symptoms in the morning, after sleep (diurnal fluctuation).

("Rarely, the movement problems associated with dopa-responsive dystonia do not appear until adulthood. In these adult-onset cases, parkinsonism usually develops before dystonia, and movement problems are slow to worsen and do not show diurnal fluctuations.")

nih.gov https://ghr.nlm.nih.gov/condition/dopa-responsive-dystonia

The next two years, well they were just amazing. Playing tennis without an issue. Walking, running, standing. In a word, living! All without pain and foot cramps. It was nothing short of a miracle. I had been freed! For a while, everything physical that was lost had somehow magically been restored back to normal. However, what I didn't realize at the time was, in my case, masking these DRD/Parkinson's disease like symptoms with any drug therapy only offers a short- term solution to this lifelong problem. It would not be too long before I'd be right back where I started - in a physical cage, with the same painful symptoms as before. And this was exactly what came to be.

After those first two freedom filled years on Sinemet, my health condition went backwards at a steady, and slow decline. The honeymoon stage was over, and now Sinemet had become a daily roller coaster of ups and downs. Eventually, I could not get out of bed in the morning without taking the drug an hour or two before I needed to get up. Also, I shook uncontrollably all the time, which I thought, was tremor from the disease itself. It was not tremor from the disease. In my case, it was dyskinesia from the medication.

(Dyskinesia refers to a category of movement disorders that are characterized by involuntary muscle movements,[1] including

movements similar to tics or chorea and diminished voluntary movements.[2] Dyskinesia can be anything from a slight tremor of the hands to an uncontrollable movement of the upper body or lower extremities. Discoordination can also occur internally especially with the respiratory muscles and it often goes unrecognized.[3] Dyskinesia is a symptom of several medical disorders that are distinguished by their underlying cause.)
wikipedia.org https://en.wikipedia.org/wiki/Dyskinesia

Management of the drug took center stage, rather than the disease itself. Over time, the pain and foot cramps came back worse than before. My denial and hiding came back as well. Truthfully, the hiding had never left my life. The longer I was on the drug, the more I recognized, just how much control I had given away. But, what other choice did I have? During this time, a person in my medical situation didn't have many options. Undaunted, I did my best to maintain myself and a positive outlook. I was beginning to see, the only thing within my control was my outlook and attitude. So I began more than ever to take enormous stock in them both.

Meanwhile, as I struggled to try to regain some of the medical traction I had made the first two years while on Sinemet, the pharmaceutical rabbit hole I went down seemed endless. One drug led to another drug, and then another. What started out as a miracle had quickly turned into a nightmare with no end in sight. All I wanted was to be normal. I thought if we could squelch the symptoms with medication, it would be as good as a cure. Right? Wrong!

What I found to be most disturbing and troubling now were these new episodes I would have which were a precursor to the foot cramping. Almost, seizure-like in nature and unlike anything I had experienced so far in my life. It was an avalanche of pain I could not escape or get out of the way of. This pain was so far beyond anything I had gone through up to this point. The first visible sign an episode was on its way, people said, they could see physical dark circles appear under my eyes. Then all hell broke loose! The excruciating foot cramps which were to follow these dark circles were not the average sitting type of cramps from years before. Nowhere near it. The pain now was so extreme, it would totally lay me out. These episodes would last at least an hour or two. Whenever I felt an episode coming on, I would fight like hell with it. Struggling not to allow it in my life or take any time away from me. This became the new norm and went on for years and years.

It had impacted and permeated every aspect of my life. From careers and relationships to hobbies and sports. Nothing in my life was left untouched by the scope of this problem. The medication I had openly invited in to ease the situation was clearly now amplifying my medical symptoms. The answers I needed to resolve this problem certainly didn't come out of a pill bottle. I would have to go far deeper in this quest to find relief to what was ailing me.

In 1991, I took a sales position with a high-tech company in Rochester, New Hampshire. It wasn't easy securing the position, but I figured if I couldn't sell them on hiring me, I didn't deserve a sales position in the first place. Working there, I met a wonderful woman and fell deeply in love with her. Shawn just took my breath away. We were quick to move in together and got engaged. Initially, no one at work, including Shawn knew about my medical situation. I cleverly did whatever necessary to hide my medical problem from the company and my fellow employees. Though, once Shawn and I moved in together, I could no longer hide this fact from her.

One day, I was experiencing one of those brutal episodes. I was lying on the floor in our bedroom on my back in great pain unable to even speak. I draped my legs over the top of the bed, trying to relieve myself from the extreme foot cramping. The pain was simply awful. Shawn laid on the bed right next to my feet, where she caressed and massaged them. Blowing on and kissing my toes, doing anything that she could do to try to relieve my pain. She loved and accepted me, in a way that I could not even fathom. Why was it so difficult to accept myself in this manner? Then it hit me like a freight train. The only person in the world not accepting of me, was me! I could not imagine that I didn't have to be alone with this any longer. The concept of not being alone with the pain and actually sharing this part of my life was completely new, foreign, and scary. This realization shocked me into a whole new approach to living. It sent me on a lifelong journey to discover how to become more accepting of myself and my disease. Could I possibly find self-acceptance through someone else's love for me? More importantly, how do I foster this love into a sincere love and self-acceptance for myself? What a discovery this was! I thought and believed back then if everything appears to be fine on the outside, that was all that mattered. My mantra would finally change as the years slowly passed. It is now this: I no longer care how things "look" on the outside. I care intensely, how things "are" on the inside. I came to adopt this philosophy and made it my own through time, and the love of a great woman.

Chapter 3 - Note to Self, "Esteem"

All the years I had spent hiding my disorder from everyone took a larger toll on me than I even recognized. It truthfully had exhausted me, mentally, emotionally, physically, and spiritually. The way I had chosen to deal with my problem had bankrupted every facet of my being. Shawn's love showed me a new path to travel. A happier and healthier way to be with it. But it wouldn't come easy. The first change I would have to make was not feeling guilty about being ill and not caring so much about how I looked to the rest of the world. In essence, addressing the biggest fear of all: what other people think of me and what they say.

It is an incredible personal undertaking to take inventory and do a self-examination of who you are at any given point in time. How I viewed myself as a person - I had never taken a serious look at before. We all have an inner voice inside of us. It highlights our weak points, silently speaking down to ourselves. I knew that voice all too well. Living with this awkward medical condition for as long as I had, fueled an endless source of counterproductive dialogue within me. Moving forward, I would need to change the way I listened to my inner voice. Acknowledging the parts of me I thought I could improve I saw as a good thing. I didn't want to shut that part of the voice down completely, but I needed to open up a new conversation with myself about recognizing the good inside me as well. The hardest part at first was seeing anything in me was worthwhile or had merit. For every five negative things my inner voice told me, I would struggle to come up with one positive trait to highlight in my mind. When I realized how hypocritical I was being to myself, things slowly improved. With a great deal of patience and repetition, over time this exercise became easier. My initial goal was to retrain my inner voice and how I internally spoke to myself, an arduous task indeed. However, I found it doable through humility, self-examination and forgiveness nonetheless.

It was this exercise which started to change me as a person. It helped me to see the negative voice inside of us never needs ammunition, but the positive voice does. I began doing tangible good deeds and other positive things in my daily life to help promote a healthier inner voice dialogue, rather than a negative one. Internal acknowledgment of these deeds and the changes associated with them was paramount, and were instrumental in bringing on necessary change. Another important factor was to minimize any sort of behaviors which might give ammunition to my negative inner voice. Through these efforts, I could see and feel a new and healthier Brian emerging.

Another piece of the puzzle I found to be a tremendous help was keeping my physical goals and dreams alive. No matter how small, no matter how crazy. The parts of us we are passionate about need to be nourished, even if they seem impossible. This is all part of maintaining our spirit and our identity.

A large part of who I am is an athlete. Perhaps, better put, one who craves athletic engagement through sport. In early fall of 1991, a friend of mine, Bob, started talking to me about ski trips to Europe. He described with fascination all the places he had been to and skied. I told him I had never been to Europe, and I thought the conversation would go no further. Remembering hearing my mom speak about her journeys through Europe, during her youth. Her face always lit up brightly whenever she spoke of it. She always said that those were the best days of her life. Bob was going through a divorce and thought it might be a good time to plan a trip like this together. I didn't have the foresight at the time, but I think we both needed to take a trip to somehow rejuvenate our spirits.

At Bob's home one evening during dinner he said to me, "You need to ski Mont Blanc with me, Brian!"

I said, "What, where?"

"The Valley Blanche would change your life forever." He then pulled out some maps of Europe and proceeded to give me a geography lesson, explaining to me that Mont Blanc was the highest peak in Europe. I thought to myself, "Change my life, hell, it would probably end my life." I must admit, Bob's enthusiasm was infectious. Though I hadn't been on skis for many years, I had never stopped dreaming about the wonderful sensation of skiing and the euphoric feeling it offers.

After the initial conversation with Bob, every time we saw each other, we would end up talking about skiing in Europe together. I don't remember how it happened, but one night after dinner, Bob said flat out to me, "I am going to Europe for a month to ski. Would you like to come with me, Brian?"

My jaw hit the floor. I explained to my friend I didn't have the proper gear or capital for a trip such as he described. "Don't worry about any of that," Bob said. "If you want to come, we can work it all out, piece by piece." He said he really needed to get away for a while, and he didn't want to go alone.

He knew some but not all of my medical shortcomings. Before we would embark on such a journey together, I would need to get him up to speed on my physical limitations, i.e. foot cramps. I told him when I skied last, I was a strong intermediate skier, but had not skied since I was 16 or 17 years old, which, at the time was more than a decade. It didn't concern him much at all. I also mentioned I could have foot cramps at any time. Again, he was undeterred.

Bob said, "Look, we will ski Mont Blanc last, and we will use the beginning stages of the trip as a warm up to getting into shape." Along the way if I don't think you can handle skiing Mont Blanc, I won't bring you up there. He also mentioned if at any point during the trip I was not comfortable with what or where we were skiing, to tell him, and he would fix it. Better still, I could go home early and not continue the trip. It sounded pretty reasonable to me. Then I asked him the biggest question of all. What happens if I get foot cramps while skiing, particularly on Mont Blanc? Bob informed me they have rescue helicopters, and he would pay for this service if I needed it. With no more excuses not to go, I was on board.

We flew into Malpensa Airport Milano, Italy in February 1992. Bob rented a car, and we set our sights on the northern Alps of Italy. Making a brief stop in Venice for a few hours, then we drove straight to Cortina d'Ampezzo. Driving into this quaint alpine village was so majestic and surreal. It was like another world which I never knew existed. The tremendous beauty and culture made an immediate impact on me. As Bob mentioned, we skied through Italy and Switzerland for the first part of the trip, then made our way to France and Chamonix. Remarkably, I had no real big issues with the skiing or the terrain. More importantly, the foot cramps had not yet reared their ugly head, which I was pleased and relieved about. I had been fastidious, about the specific times I took my Sinemet, and it looked like it was paying off, so far. Our skiing warm up included Cortina d'Ampezzo, Cervinia, and Zermatt. It was definitely way bigger skiing than I had ever experienced in the Northeast, by a long shot. So far, I had handled myself competently with the skiing and thought perhaps Mont Blanc would not be so bad.

In just a few short days, the Vallee Blanche on Mont Blanc with all its dangers would be staring me right in the face. This part of the trip's success was dependent on having good and clear weather. We certainly didn't want to be facing any sort of serious or inclement weather obstacles during our descent. I heard from Bob through our many conversations about this mountain say skiers far better than I had good reasons to fear Mont Blanc. I made note of it, being one of those among the many who feared skiing it and I acutely respected the dangers this challenge posed.

Bob had used the phrase: "There is death on that mountain," when I first asked him to describe it to me. I asked him what he meant by, "DEATH"? He went on to say, first of all there could be avalanches. The biggest risk to any skier, Bob said, while making the descent back down to Chamonix are the crevasses. This was about a four-hour journey, all of which was out-of-bounds skiing. Most of the folks who ski the Vallee Blanche employ a ski guide. This helps them to make a safe descent and avoid the hazards and pitfalls of skiing this treacherous mountain.

The morning of the Mont Blanc run, I had turned myself inside out with fear. I'd worked myself into such a tizzy about it I had become a complete mess. My stomach was churning with worry. Ten to fifteen trips to the bathroom proved I wasn't dealing very well with the stress of what lay ahead of me. One of these trips to the bathroom, during breakfast, suddenly ignited a light foot cramping episode. Nothing all too serious. I sat on the floor in the bathroom and massaged both of my feet for a few minutes. Then the cramp quickly subsided. I returned to the breakfast table as if nothing even happened. Before I could take my seat to rejoin Bob at the table, he said," Time to go. So," we both grabbed our gear and set off to Chamonix.

I had followed my friend blindly to Europe, to ski the Vallee Blanche, mostly because he said it would change my life. I honestly had no idea the ways in which it could or would change my life, but I believed him. Arriving in Chamonix, Bob's urging me to come now made immediate sense. There it was, lying right before me. I recall Bob pulling me aside and asking me what I thought. When he asked me, I realized my fear had now been replaced with exuberance and excitement. This experience and the day that lay ahead of me would undoubtedly be epic. The only true fear haunting me in my life has been, "being alive, and not living." There was just no way I was going to let my inner demons or personal fears tarnish the potential of this opportunity.

This journey life had in store for me would be realized on this day.

We took the two-stage cable car ride to the top of the Aiguille du Midi as the village of Chamonix disappeared beneath us. The awe-inspiring lift to the summit of Mont Blanc was nothing less than breathtaking. As the second cable car reached the summit platform we disembarked, entering a brilliant blue glacial ice cave. Walking through the cave was exactly like walking into a shimmering sapphire. Sparkling vividly, refracting the light as we made our way through. Emerging from the blue icy tunnel for the first time I saw the challenge that lay ahead. An enormously sketchy repel leading to a valley as endless as a sea. Bob turned to me and smiled with eager eyes. I looked back at him confidently and smiled too. Without hesitation, I said, "Bob, I can do this." He asked, "Are you sure?" I affirmed my commitment with a huge smile. Yes!

Holding our skis and poles in one hand and carefully side stepping the steep incline, we made our way down the side of the alp. Not for the faint of heart, I can assure you. The sky was such a deep blue against an ocean of white snow, it almost hurt to even look at it. After a twenty to thirty minute repel with ski boots on down the side of the alp, we arrived at the plateau where we could put our skis on.

With my heart pounding adrenaline, I stepped into my ski bindings and watched Bob drop into the steepest section we had seen this entire trip. I must admit, I was intimidated! It was now my turn to start the journey and drop in. Paralyzed with fear, I didn't make one turn to scrub off speed. I was scared and frozen stiff. My legs wouldn't move. By the time I made it to the bottom of the section, I was going way too fast. Impacting a large mogul, I then took the biggest wipe out. What a total whiteout, wipe out! Covered with snow, I looked just like a snowman. Letting out a loud, echoing "Wahooooooo," so Bob would know I was alright. I gave myself a once over to make sure I was not hurt. As I made it to my feet, it felt like all of France was laughing at me. For the very first time in my life, I didn't care. Look where I was and what I was doing. I felt blessed to even be there, and this now became my new focus. Skiing over to me, Bob asked, "Are you OK?" He looked extremely concerned. We had limited daylight to successfully get off the mountain. My start didn't inspire much confidence in my friend. I told him I was fine and I just needed to get that out of my system.

With that behind me, the Vallee Blanche opened up to an enormous snowfield. We danced gracefully down the Vallee on the fresh powder, provided from the night before. If there was a heaven on earth, we had found it.

Carving big "S" turns down the gentle Vallee slope, with the massive European Alps surrounding us. It didn't feel real to me. It was as though I were in a dream. This far exceeded any skiing experience I have ever had before, or since. However, reality would set back in soon enough.

The snowfield went on for it seemed like miles. With the effortless terrain and powder behind us, we had skied further into the Vallee Blanche where the slope and pitch was steadily increasing. The Vallee and its glacier were narrowly winding and switching back down Mont Blanc. Also, the skiing was getting more technical, scratchy, and treacherous. Pretty soon, I found myself in way over my head. My skiing ability had been stretched to its limits. I told myself, "Where you have to do a stem christie or snow plow to survive, do it!" If I wanted to live through this experience, I would have to put my ego in check and forget about looking cool as I skied down. This new strategy was a slower, less fluid, safer descent. However, my lack of progress was eating up precious time that we really couldn't afford. Bob would ski ahead and wait for me. When I caught up with him, off he'd go again to lead the way.

Eventually, the narrow part of this gigantic Vallee, which was the only safe part to ski on, looked to be changing again. Skiing along on a switchback, the path seemed as though it was opening up. I could no longer see Bob, and I thought to myself, "This can't be good." Continuing on this icy scratchy path, I start to see why Bob had disappeared. Right before me lay an enormous cliff edge, nothing but ice, huge moguls, and frankly the gnarliest piece of terrain I had ever encountered on skis. I turned away from the problem, hitting the brakes to stop. When I did that, the angle of the previous switchback I was skiing on turned me around backwards. I now was stuck with the tails of my skis lodged in a mogul facing up the Vallee Blanche. I struggled and struggled to free myself, with no reward. All the while I kept trying to push my way up Mont Blanc, but I could not break free of its hold.

The minutes were like hours, and I was becoming exhausted. Then finally, with all my might I pushed one more time, and I was able to free myself from such a compromising position. When I got myself turned around, I was facing the exact same problem I was before. Bob was waiting for me at the bottom of this hellish section. Furious, I shouted, "Why didn't you tell me?" He was so far away from me it took a moment for my transmission to reach his ears. Again I yelled, "Why didn't you tell me?" I saw Bob put his hands to the sides of his mouth, so to direct his voice right at me. I could see his mouth moving, but his words took a few moments to make a connection with my ears. Then I heard, with crystal-clear clarity, "Because you would have never come," he yelled. He was right! Instantly, I felt my anger with Bob turned into sheer will and determination to make it past this section and off the mountain safely. I took my time, breaking the challenge up into very small segments. Making the task of skiing this impossible section for me doable. Little by little, I chipped away at the section, skiing with more and more control. Gaining confidence, I reached the bottom where Bob was waiting for me. "No time to celebrate, Brian," he said. "We have to make tracks!" I watched as he set off, and I immediately followed him into another snowfield open section.

I remember thinking to myself I had gone through so many emotions on this descent already. Fear, adjuration, joy, hate, anger. The Vallee wasn't just challenging me on a physical level, it was challenging my emotions as well. It allowed me to recognize in myself, through my own physical hardships, hiding from those hardships would never change them. They would always be there waiting for me, until I was ready to turn and face them directly. This day I found the joy in accepting one of life's challenges and realized that I could no longer keep hiding with my own physical issues. Furthermore, the Vallee was teaching me that I was capable of facing these challenges. When we choose to hide from our insecurities, it only serves to punctuate the weaknesses we're trying so desperately to conceal.

There were a great deal more eventful circumstances on our descent that added to the charm of the Mont Blanc experience. It was truly life in a day. I recall feeling invigorated while skiing back down into Chamonix. More than I had felt before, my spirit was now alive in a way that was completely new to me. I had been awakened! How fortunate I was. Close to a four-and-a-half-hour physical journey, and my medication, miraculously had held up for the entire descent. In fact, I felt so wonderfully alive upon reaching the bottom of Mont Blanc, Bob asked me if I would like him to pick me up with the car. I thanked him for the offer and said I would rather walk back to the car with him. "We made it this far together, I am sure I can make it the rest of the way," I said. Bob just smiled at me. Which was the sum of our celebration, and it was enough.

There is an empowerment that comes with a commitment to the unknown. Taking a leap of faith in yourself for most of us doesn't happen every day. However, there are many opportunities we let go by from time to time, without fully knowing what we are missing out on. Being out there participating in life, is the opportunity to be reborn, as it was for me the day I skied

Mont Blanc. I shudder to think how different I would be today if I had decided not to ski. What a huge part of myself, and a chapter in my life, I would have missed out on.

Summit of Mont Blanc, France.

Me (left) & Bob (right)

February 1992

Chapter 4 - The Lost and Found Years

Upon returning home from Europe, I could see this trip changed me for the better. I had grown in ways that would take me years to realize. It had given me a confidence and a self-assurance which up until this point had been a missing part of who I was. All the spiritual gifts I had received from Mont Blanc and the European experience would take time to root and foster personal growth.

During this period in time, Shawn and I parted company. As sad as it was, I knew it was the right thing for the both of us. And she agreed. I decided to take a new sales position with a high-tech company in Seattle, Washington. It was successful, but short-lived due to my declining health. The medication was failing to be an effective tool to manage my symptoms any longer. It was now taking much too long for the drug to kick in and start working in the morning. Plus, its duration and effectiveness were on the decline too. With the painful, seizure-like episodes becoming more and more frequent, I didn't know where to turn. So, again I turned inward.

Chronic and extreme pain has a way of molding and shaping your being. It's an undeniable force while you attempt to oppose it, identical to swift water over time, carving out canyons and shaping rock. This was what these painful episodes were trying to do to my spirit. Mold and reshape it, through extreme physical pain. I wondered how much this disease would take from me. The mere thought of it scared me to death. Probably because I had no idea what the answer might be. Besides the symptoms worsening, the side effects from the drugs themselves were getting out of control too. Whenever weather changes or any sort of fluctuation in barometric pressure occurred, it would send me into a tailspin. It felt like a sumo wrestler was sitting on my head. I was sluggish, with brain fog, unable to get out of my own way. It was horribly debilitating. Also, my sleep pattern had been drastically interrupted and wasn't healthy at all. I was quickly moving into the direction of an insomniac's way of life, with no recourse or thoughts on how to correct the issue. The violent shaking was constant and exhausting. My legs never stopped involuntarily moving while on the medication. At the time, I thought it was simple tremor from the disease. It wasn't, it was dyskinesia from the medications as I previously mentioned. I had heard from some medical resource in the early 1990s state the human brain can only make natural dopamine while the body is in REM sleep. I had no idea if it were true or not. All I knew was if this statement were true I couldn't be making any dopamine during a 24-hour period because at the time, I was hardly sleeping at all, day or night. It was a greatly concerning period in my life.

There is an enormous amount of research material on the subject of sleep and dopamine available online these days. I found much of it contrasting in nature and confusing. Time continually advances, as it does it will inevitably reveal changes through research. Regardless, these differences of opinions I encountered while researching this subject, left me scratching my head a bit. I invite you to draw your own conclusions while doing your personal research.

Volkow et al. "Evidence That Sleep Deprivation Downregulates Dopamine D2R in Ventral Striatumin the Human Brain" Journal of Neuroscience, 2012. There are lots of signs that point toward the involvement of the neurotransmitter dopamine in wakefulness. Drugs that increase levels of dopamine in brain (including, but not limited to, drugs like cocaine, amphetamine, meth, and Ritalin) also increase feelings of wakefulness. Increasing dopamine in the brain via genetic alterations, like getting rid of the dopamine transporter in a mouse, stopping dopamine from getting recycled, produces a mouse that sleeps less. Diseases that are characterized by low dopamine levels, like Parkinsons, also have daytime sleepiness. But a neurotransmitter is only as good as its receptor. Dopamine has two main types of receptors, and the current hypothesis is that the wakefulness promoting effects of dopamine may be controlled partially by the D2 type receptor. Antipsychotics, which block D2 type receptors, make people sleepy, and previous studies showed decreased D2 binding in the brains of sleep deprived people. But the question is: what is causing the decreases in D2 when people are sleep deprived? The authors of this study hypothesized that this was due to increased dopamine release, which would cause decreases in D2 receptors (this is a basic idea in pharmacology, when a group of receptors is overstimulated, some receptors will leave the membrane, making the membrane less sensitive to stimulation).To test this hypothesis, they took a bunch of human volunteers, and either sleep deprived them overnight (they kept them in a facility with a nurse bugging them to keep their eyes open if they got drowsy), or kept them in the facility to get a good night's rest (all participants underwent both conditions). In the morning, they looked at the D2 receptors in the striatum of the brain, an area with loads of dopamine and associated with things like arousal and reward. To do this, they used positron emission tomography (PET), which uses a radioactive tracer (C-raclopride), which binds to D2 type receptors, allowing you to see how many are present. They showed that D2 type receptor binding was definitely lower in sleep deprived people. But what does this mean? Does it mean that there's more dopamine release when you're tired, decreasing the D2 type receptors? Or do the D2 type receptors decrease for some other reason? To look at this, the authors of the study treated the participants with methylphenidate (Ritalin), which increased the amounts of dopamine. They hypothesized that if sleep deprivation produced more dopamine release, the methylphenidate should produce larger increases in dopamine than in well rested patients.

scientificamerican.com https://blogs.scientificamerican.com/
scicurious-brain/sleep-deprived-mind-your-dopamine/

The seizure-like cramps had progressed to the point where working a full-time job became impossible. I had grown, reliably unreliable. Blinding headaches, foot cramping, lying on the floor with writhing pain all had become daily occurrences. After realizing my chosen career in high-tech sales was over, I found this pill intensely hard to swallow. Back then, I believed strongly what I did for a living defined who I was as a person. Today, I see it much differently. Fortunately, I had some money saved up and bought myself some time with it.

I needed to invest myself, in something which could help heal my spirit, while my body was seemingly falling apart. So, I began to once again, gravitate toward music. I would lose myself in the rapture I felt whenever I played, wrote, or sang these songs of my own creation. The power of music again was saving my life. It became the outlet and medium which I aspired to be known for. It made me feel safe, not alone and productive. Every day started out and ended the exact same way. Writing music, playing music, recording music, and singing music.

It was soon after I left my career in high-tech sales I began volunteering at the local junior high school teaching songwriting. They had developed a special program for outside artists to bring their talents and abilities into the school to share with the student body. It could not have come at a more appropriate time in my life. My days were filled with sharing my intense love of music with the students. Quite surprisingly, none of the students seemed to care at all about my illness, my physical symptoms, or limitations. Even though, I shook violently most of the time and had my foot cramping episodes, still the students supported me fully. I found an acceptance, appreciation, and respect from them, as they did from me. There was a healthy, even exchange between the students and myself. On many levels, it made the entire experience highly rewarding. So much so in fact, I developed an artist in residence program called Sound Awakenings. I would go to schools all over New England, using music as the vehicle to get youngsters to step outside their comfort zones. The program promoted personal growth through music. We wrote songs and shared our most inner thoughts then recorded our creative ideas. I wanted to show the kids there was something worthwhile developing in each one of us. Those music classrooms were our safe place. We freed ourselves from our internal fears which might stop us and cause us to hide. In the beginning, I thought what a gift I was sharing with these young students. Truth be told, I received far more from them than they ever got from me. Their courage, trust, and acceptance brought me to another level in my own personal development. How they opened up to me was a shining example of strength I so badly needed in my life at this time. Plus, their love and acceptance of me helped to further illustrate the fact I still had some internal work to do on myself in this department.

As the years passed and my health further and further declined, Sound Awakenings became too overwhelming for me to continue. Moving the recording equipment, instruments, amps, and other miscellaneous parts that were necessary for the program sadly had exceeded the limits of my physical ability. Not to mention, playing my instrument was getting more and more challenging. It was becoming exceedingly difficult for me to play my guitar at the level in which I had been accustomed to. Yet again, I heard the question rattling around in my head. How much will this disease take from me - to which, I still had no answer.

When Sound Awakenings ended, my physical health had deteriorated to a level where even leaving the house became difficult. Shockingly, out of the blue, a new symptom had developed to accompany the litany of others I had already been dealing with. While walking, I would get the sensation like I was losing my balance and then fall to my knees. It started out more like a controlled fall, so as not to really hurt myself by falling backwards. In the beginning, this strange development seemed to happen mostly while I was walking through doors. The tight space would feel as if it were closing in on me. Then it grew into other areas, wherever I happened to feel closed in, or a confined situation, perhaps in a crowd of people. It was a very unnerving symptom to deal with and an even more unnerving symptom to witness. It quite frankly frightened and shocked the onlooker, highlighting quite clearly, with even more visual impact, my physical woes.

Besides the sudden falling to my knees, I was also starting to experience freezing when I walked. It was as if my brain shut down for a moment, unable to calculate or measure the next step. My gait was becoming more limited too. Shortened strides, not picking up my feet and doing the Parkinson's shuffle, were all signs I was receding backwards with my health. Similar to the falling to my knees, the freezing was brought on when I had objects like doorways, and thresholds in my path. My brain just could not calculate or handle those types of scenarios.

A common symptom experienced by people with Parkinson's disease (PD) is "freezing": a sudden, but temporary, inability to move. It can happen at any time, such as when walking (called a freezing gait) or when attempting to rise from a seated position. Freezing episodes seem to occur primarily when initiating movement or navigating around obstacles. The exact cause of freezing is unknown, although sometimes it occurs when the person is due for their next dose of medication.[1,2]

Negative consequences of freezing:

Freezing episodes limit the mobility of a person with PD and may contribute to reduced socialization and a lower quality of life. In addition, freezing can be dangerous and is associated with falls in people with PD. Approximately 38% of people with PD fall each year, and freezing increases the risk of falls as freezing occurs without warning. Falls can cause additional health problems, including broken bones or head injury.1,2

Techniques to overcome freezing:

Physical therapy and occupational therapy can be helpful to reduce or overcome freezing episodes. Physical therapy focuses on the physical rehabilitation of people recovering from injuries or disease with the goal of restoring mobility, as well as educating patients on managing their condition to maintain long-term benefits. Occupational therapy also deals with rehabilitation and motion but is focused more on enabling the person to engage in daily activities as seamlessly as possible. Occupational therapists also suggest adaptations and modifications to the person's environment.3

There are several techniques that can help people with PD overcome freezing, including:

· Use music. Humming or singing a song while walking to the rhythm can help keep you moving.

· Try a metronome. Metronomes keep a steady beat, and walking to the beat can help reduce freezing.

· Change direction. If you can't move straight ahead, try stepping to the side first, or take a step back, before going forward.

· Shift your weight from side to side before attempting a step can help initiate movement.

· March in place, lifting your knees as high as you can, before stepping forward.

· Move another part of your body. If your legs won't move, swing your arms first and then try moving your legs again.

· Imagine a line in front of you. Visualize a line in front of you and step over it. For spots in the house that are consistently tricky, like a doorway, you can use tape on the floor to create a line to step over.

· Use a laser pointer. Shine the laser in front of you and step on or over it.

· Ask for help. Ask a friend or family member for a gentle nudge.

· Practice dancing. The movements of dance are rhythmic and can help strengthen your balance and fluidity.

· Exercise in intervals. Interval training on a stationary bike involves changing the direction or rate of activity. This can help improve strength and motor functioning.1,2,4,5

As with any symptom, patients who experience freezing episodes should mention this to their neurologist who is managing their care. The neurologist may make changes to medication or provide a referral to a physical or occupational therapist.
parkinsonsdisease.net https://parkinsonsdisease.net/living-with-pd/overcoming-freeze/

It was during these darkest years I took some time to reflect and attempt to heal myself from within. My physical abilities were depleted more, day by day. The life I knew, which had always been somewhat unpredictable, had been reduced to almost a standstill. At this time, as far as my pain level went, everything was on ten. Brutal! The seizure episodes had gotten so violent and bad I seldom left my room. As bad as the seizures were, through the years I had learned, instead of fighting with the pain, I would meditate away from it. I found this to be relaxing and helpful at the same time. It helped to shorten the duration of the episodes and reduced my stress about having them. Whenever, I felt a seizure-like episode coming on, I would calmly lie down with it. Now, I resisted the urge to fight back with the pain, allowing it to wash over me like a wave. This approach was a drastic change from when I first encountered these crippling episodes, with much healthier results. Going away mentally until the pain subsided rather than trying to fight with it, was a revelation years in the making.

I continued to write and record my music. Refusing to give up playing the guitar or composing because of this disease. Holding on, I kept struggling to maintain this goal for as long as I could. Now, the dexterity in my hands was being adversely affected by the disease. I could see that it was only a matter of time before this part of me, like many of my other passions, might be silenced too.

There, off in the distance of my mind, reverberated the question that had continued to plague me throughout the years. How much will this disease take from me. A question which haunted me for far too long. In the silence of my darkest thoughts, I pondered its complexities. Sitting quietly listening to myself I sought out an answer. After an undetermined amount of time, it came to me.

This disease can take absolutely everything from me. And it just might! However, if I intentionally don't allow the pain of what I am going through with this disorder to touch my spirit or my soul, then it can't completely have me. I can maintain my spirit and keep the best parts of myself alive. This notion was a new beginning towards the self acceptance I was seeking. From this point forward, I felt like I was truly safe from losing everything that I am.

Parkinson's disease, and all the years I went through living in pain with it, made me realize there isn't a soul on earth who doesn't struggle with some form of pain. Some pain you can see, and some you can't. I learned if you allow any form of pain - physical, emotional, mental, or spiritual - touch your spirit or soul it will damage you far more than the pain itself ever could. There is an enormous relief and power that comes to a person when first they realize they have the control and choice - the choice to decide whether you allow your pain to damage your spirit or not. This knowledge granted me instant control and empowerment at a point in time in my life where everything else was beyond my control. So how much will this disease take from me? I still don't have the answer to this question. Regardless of how much it may, or may not take, this much I can promise you. I will never allow my physical pain or any pain I suffer from for that matter, damage my spirit. Not ever!

When my medical symptoms started to impede on my physical abilities as a guitarist, I knew I could wait no longer. Something had to be done. I may not have any medical recourse, but maybe there was another way to abate this situation. The biggest issue I was having was with my guitar of choice, the Fender Stratocaster, was a notoriously difficult guitar to play. I was having trouble chording and rhythmically keeping time. Now when I played, it seemed as though the guitar was fighting against me, rather than playing with me. It became my mission to make guitars play easier, so I could prolong my ability to play. The guitar, as popular as it is, can be viewed as a difficult instrument to play. Not the most difficult, but by no means easy. The coordination it takes between hands to play accurately and cleanly takes years of practice to master. This was one part of me I wouldn't give up. Not without a fight!

One day, I was lying on the floor in pain, as I often did back then, having one of my medical moments. Letting the pain wash over me, I noticed my Strat right beside me on the floor. As I sighted the neck and headstock, I saw a bow in the neck. Then I depressed the tremolo bar and could not believe my eyes. What I saw instantly changed my understanding of guitars forever. Not only did I see the headstock move, which you would expect, I also saw it twisting as it moved. It was then I realized for the very first time why it was so difficult for me to play my instrument. Because lying there, my guitar was in as much physical pain as I was. My disability became an ability. An ability to see, feel, and relate to stringed instruments and the pain they feel. If a guitar has a difficult time maintaining its physical shape under string tension, said guitar will be a very difficult guitar to play. The research and work I did enabled me to continue to play the guitar at a high level - or at least a similar level as before the disease impaired my skills as a guitarist.

This discovery led me to two U.S. patents for guitar technology in the late '90s and early 2000s. Moving forward, this was only the beginning. I pitched my discovery to Fender Guitars. After all, I had an extensive background in corporate sales and felt very at home in this particular world. After many conversations and numerous questions, Fender and I set up a meeting at the NAMM show in Nashville, Tennessee. Fender agreed to sign a non-disclosure Agreement, (NDA) with me, after which, we would set up a time for me to go to Scottsdale, Arizona to disclose my invention to the Fender Guitars executives at the world headquarters.

This was a pretty big deal. The vice president I met at the NAMM show, Mike Lewis, said this rarely happens with inventors and Fender Guitars. Mike told me I was 1 percent of 1 percent of the people who ever get this far into Fender. So I embarked on this opportunity with the intensity I thought it deserved. We agreed I would have close to a year to prepare. Knowing the task ahead of me, I buckled down and wasted no time getting started. The presentation I ultimately prepared for Fender Guitars took every bit of that year to complete.

By this time, I was a full-blown insomniac, sleeping maybe ten to fifteen hours a week. I spent countless hours immersed in control studies with the guitar while the rest of the time, my PowerPoint presentation was front burner. When I wasn't working on the guitar, I was writing about it. Besides my dedication to my invention, I still wrote and recorded my music. I never took a break! To say I was living an extraordinarily unhealthy, out-of-balanced lifestyle was to put it mildly. I never slept, my diet was horrible, and the weight I was gaining, just wasn't like me.

More than at any other time in my life, I had started to identify with myself as being a tragically, unhealthy person. Up to this point, I had always taken great pride in how I took care of myself. Yes, I had this horrible disease and circumstance to live with, but I had not ever let myself go, not ever. I didn't smoke or drink alcohol, nor have I ever done drugs of any kind. In retrospect, I believe it was fear which motivated my decision-making back then. The fear of inviting another issue, like drugs or alcohol into my already out of control life. Because the prescription drugs I had been taking for years, I believed was clouding my judgment more than I even realized. Looking back on those days, I now view my behavior remarkably similar to those of an addict. I can see now I had fallen into a place where I knew I wasn't driving my life. My life was driving me. It was only a matter of time before it would catch up to me and all come crashing down.

While I watched my life spiral out of control, it felt as though I was a man on a mission, running out of time. Knowing how much I had to prepare for the Fender project and running at the pace I had set for myself, could only spell disaster. My fear of being nothing because of my medical situation was the crop that kept spurring me onward. I had lost so much in the way of my life, I had committed to giving this guitar invention my absolute complete and total attention. And that was exactly what I was doing.

When the meeting with Fender Guitars in Scottsdale, Arizona came along, I was functioning on sheer will and determination. The meeting itself went fine. However, I somehow knew after I had disclosed the true nature of my invention to Mike Lewis and the other gentlemen in the meeting Fender Guitars would not be buying my invention. This first patent was based on a new way of tuning a Stratocaster or any tremolo type of guitar. It was considered a methodology patent. Everyone, including Mike Lewis was blown away by how well it worked at the NAMM show, a year earlier. While Mr. Lewis was intrigued and awe struck by its functionality, he didn't see how Fender could successfully implement it as a viable addition to their product line. There was no new hardware or anything to add to the guitar with what I had created or showed them at this time.

Undeterred and with great resolve, I came back home and immediately began doing research. My goal was to find a way to make some hardware pieces for the guitar that would automate my methodology patent process. Not an easy task! However, after numerous control studies and countless hours of research, I developed my first piece of hardware and patented it about a year after the Fender Guitar meeting. Once I had finished my work on the new piece of hardware for the guitar, it was as if I smacked into a brick wall. I was stopped dead in my tracks! I simply had nothing more left to give, and my tank, was empty.

Drained, and with nothing more left inside of me, the physical box surrounding me was closing in on my life. Continuing, day by day, shrinking its parameters, thus, reducing me and the quality of my life in the process. I had to stop my research and work with guitars. My symptoms and pain levels were worse than ever before. I really didn't think it was possible, but it was.

As bad as things were physically at the time, I never felt defeated, which I was grateful for. Through it all, I always somehow maintained a strong positive mental attitude. I'm not sure where it came from, but I had been this way since I was a young child. It proved to be my saving grace. I suppose I had learned early on from everything I had been through, the only thing anyone of us can control is our attitude.

While the guitar invention and my music certainly fed my spirit and kept me going, I eventually recognized that it took just as much away from me as it gave. The time, energy, and extreme effort that these disciplines took to achieve any sort of success in, for years diverted my attention away from any kind of focus on my health issues. Better said, doing anything proactive to help my medical situation was not foremost in my mind during these days. Surviving the pain and being as productive as I could be had been my only immediate concern. This sonic wave which I had been riding on for most of my life, now was coming to an abrupt end.

Chapter 5 - Finding Balance

Balance is an incredibly difficult thing to achieve, and even harder to maintain. I believe to find a balance in your life, you first have to see and acknowledge how far out of balance you are to start with. In my case, this took time and reflection. Then I could identify and recognize the parts of me responsible for pulling me out of balance. Once I had identified those issues, I could address them, one by one, thus, bringing my life back into a better balance.

After the guitar invention period, I felt a bit rudderless. For the first time in many years, I didn't have a direction. Regardless, I had little energy or inclination to invest in anything. The disease and its pain was all consuming and had me under its control. The result was I had become stagnant.

One of the issues which I noticed pulling me out of balance was my long-term use of medications. I could tell I had reached a level of toxicity through my years of use. I had never noticed before, but now my urine was a deep burnt-orange color and smelled horrible. My eyes, ears, and nose secreted a pungent stale odor - all signs I took as being toxic on the medications. Interestingly enough, another drug I had been prescribed by Dr. Palmer for my Parkinson's was called Permax. When I started taking this new wonder drug, Dr. Palmer told me it could help augment the effectiveness of the Sinemet and may even arrest the advancement of Parkinson's disease. Which sounded helpful to my situation, so without question, I started taking the drug. While on this drug Permax, I didn't notice any difference in my symptoms or find any benefit whatsoever. It was, in a word nebulous to me.

Maybe 15 to 18 years after being prescribed permax, I read Permax had the potential to cause heart valve failure in the patients who took the drug. This blew my mind! I called my neurologist at the time, Dr. Shabbir Abbasi at New England Neurological. He told me I would need to get an ultrasound of my heart to see if there could be any damage from ingesting the drug, which I had been taking for a substantial amount of time. I took his advice and thank god, there wasn't any heart damage. When I called Dr. Abbasi back to let him know my heart was fine and that I would be discontinuing the drug, his response was, "You can't quit the drug cold turkey. You could die." To which I explained, "Well, this is a distinct possibility regardless of what I do in the situation I am in." I felt I was responsible for myself being in this position because I hadn't done my due diligence and researched the drug like I had for Sinemet. I implicitly trusted the word of my physician Dr. Palmer and left it at that. Dr. Palmer wasn't at fault in guiding me towards Permax. He was kindly passing along information which he was told by the pharmaceutical company at the time. Besides, there wasn't a ton of options for me to choose from at this juncture. I believe this proves how vitally important it is to check and read all the medication side effects before committing to any drug therapy program. In addition, it proves how dangerous any drug therapy can be. When it was all said and done, I quit the Permax, cold turkey. I feel so fortunate not to have suffered any complications or additional side effects from the time I had taken this "wonder drug." Permax was eventually taken off the market by the FDA and discontinued as a viable drug therapy for Parkinson's disease.

Pergolide (marketed as Permax) FDA today announces that manufacturers of pergolide drug products, which are used to treat Parkinson's disease, will voluntarily remove these drugs from the market because of the risk of serious damage to patients' heart valves.
fda.gov https://www.fda.gov/drugs/postmarket-drug-safety-information-patients-and-providers/pergolide-marketed-permax-information

I began to take notice. It was not only the disease itself negatively impacting my life, but the medications I was using to combat the symptoms of the disease as well. Through the years, the drug therapy approach had bought me some time, but at what cost? It became apparent to me I could go no further on the medication roller coaster. One of the most mysterious characteristics of this neurological disorder, I understand now to be, is treatment. Rare if ever, are two individuals stricken in the exact same way. Yet, the drug therapy treatments are all basically the same. We as individuals with Parkinson's disease are afflicted in a unique, symptomatic way specific to us. So how does it make any sense to have such a specific, broad-based drug therapy approach to neurological diseases which promote such different and unique symptoms in so many patients? It just boggles my mind.

Around this time, 2004, stem cell research was a seriously controversial and hot topic. For a person in my medical situation, the hope this subject brought me was immeasurable. The buzz around my town in the early fall was Senator, John Kerry and Michael J. Fox were holding a meeting at the high school on embryonic stem cell research. My brother Mark and I both attended this over-capacity event. Wouldn't you know it. My old basketball coach, Coach Ford, saw me and my brother at the front door attempting to access the event without preregistration, or event tickets. He took matters into his own hands and ushered us right in the school. Coach Ford sat my brother in the audience, then he found me a seat right on the stage near Michael J. Fox and Senator John Kerry. The coach knew how important it was for us to be there. He saw to it we were not only there, but a part of the event.

At some point during the meeting, I raised my hand to make a comment, and the Senator from Massachusetts approached me with the microphone. My comment was "Hope is something we all need to hold on to, whether it be false hope or otherwise." I went on to add I'd much rather hold on to hope than be residual income to the pharmaceutical industry for the rest of my life. Because in my mind, this is exactly what I had become - a prisoner not only to the disease but to the medications as well.

This was a time of enormous debate between the Bush White House and what Senator Kerry was proposing. Stem cell research could promise a cure for not only Parkinson's but other awful and debilitating diseases too. The brouhaha was President Bush had limited the funding for embryonic stem cell research. If elected to the office of president, Kerry promised to lift the current Bush ban on embryonic stem cell research, and he would devote $100 million of federal aid yearly to fund this program.

Kerry lost the election that year to Bush. Then it was as if the promise of a miraculous stem cell cure went all but silent. At least for the Parkinson's patients in this part of the world, the stem cell buzz had dissipated far too soon for patients hopeful for real answers.

This stem cell development stumped me. Being of the opinion when you're not sure what to do, the best recourse is to do nothing. Well, this is what I did. Nothing!

I did nothing for as long as I could bare it. It was then I realized, taking no form of action would yield no results. If I were serious about breaking out of this prison, then I was going to have to do more than I had been. Doing nothing, I saw was no longer a viable option. My brother Mark, told me about this operation called deep brain stimulation, DBS. Brain surgery sure didn't sound like a minor approach to my problem. Truthfully, the notion scared the hell out of me. The name of a neurosurgeon and his impressive reputation came through my brother Mark. His name was Dr. Bruce Cook. He was renowned in our area as a highly skilled neurosurgeon and had performed surgery on Michael J. Fox. So, this information put my mind at ease a bit, but it still was brain surgery. I quickly made an appointment to discuss the procedure and anything else I could think of about what this surgery may entail. After meeting with Dr. Cook, I was still petrified about moving forward with the operation. I couldn't pull the trigger. As bad as my health was, I felt at this time it was too intrusive. After all, this wasn't a haircut which would grow back. I needed to take some time to give all the possibilities careful consideration. Before leaving Dr. Cook's office, I shared with him my feelings and told him I would not be moving forward with the operation at this time. What impressed me the most about him was how understanding he was about my concerns. He agreed it was a big decision. He told me to take all the time I needed to think it over. And if I needed him or had any questions, to call him back, so we could talk further on the subject. He was enormously relaxed about it all, applying no pressure, and I found this to be one of his most impressive qualities thus far.

About a year or so had passed since our initial meeting, and I could see the writing on the wall. My condition and the quality of my life had only gotten worse. This had been the pattern for a long time now. I decided I wanted to move forward with Dr. Cook and the DBS operation. I thought skiing Mont Blanc was scary, and it was. But it was nothing like the fear and worry I felt about having this operation. One of the biggest reasons I had decided to go through with the surgery was because it came with the promise of a likely decrease in the medications I was on. At this point, it made enough sense to me to want to move forward. The other big reason why I chose Dr. Cook was his implementation and procedure for this surgery. Dr. Cook provided his patients a one-day solution to DBS surgery. He didn't break the surgeries up into different stages like some of the other local doctors did. I saw this as an enormous advantage and benefit to me as a patient. Most other neurosurgeons in my area broke the procedure up into three different and separate operations, over ninety days. Dr. Cook's procedure eliminated the risk of infection by two-thirds compared to the other surgeons. This was a huge factor in my decision-making.

The morning of the surgery, my dear friend Jean and I made our way to the hospital. I was brought into the facility in a wheelchair at 6:00 a.m., October 5, 2007. Dr. Cook requested I go off my medication the day before the surgery. This insured Dr. Cook would have the best opportunity to visually see how I reacted to the placement of the stimulators. After a nine-hour bilateral DBS surgery on Friday, I walked out two days later on Sunday afternoon. From the moment, I entered the surgical daycare pre-op until my release on Sunday I had zero pain. None! Not even a headache, which I found to be amazing. The only issue I had with the entire operation was a negative post-operative response to the anesthesia. I threw up a few times, and that was it! The targeted region of my brain Dr. Cook implanted the stimulators was the sub-thalamic nucleus - a region, in the brain about the same size as a pea. (I know what you're thinking, "Pea brain.") He had mentioned to me briefly I may feel some physical benefits from the stimulators being implanted there. Remarkably enough, I did.

The subthalamic nucleus is a small lens-shaped nucleus in the brain where it is, from a functional point of view, part of the basal ganglia system. In terms of anatomy, it is the major part of the subthalamus. As suggested by its name, the subthalamic nucleus is located ventral to the thalamus. It is also dorsal to the substantia nigra and medial to the internal capsule. It was first described by Jules Bernard Luys in 1865,[1] and the term *corpus Luysi* or *Luys' body* is still sometimes used. wikipedia.org https://en.wikipedia.org/wiki/Subthalamic_nucleus

Subthalamic Nucleus Deep Brain Stimulation (STN DBS) is a well-established and effective treatment modality for selected patients with Parkinson's disease (PD). Since its advent, systematic exploration of the effect of stimulation parameters including the stimulation intensity, frequency, and pulse width have been carried out to establish optimal therapeutic ranges. This review examines published data on these stimulation parameters in terms of efficacy of treatment and adverse effects. Altering stimulation intensity is the mainstay of titration in DBS programming via alterations in voltage or current settings, and is characterized by a lower efficacy threshold and a higher side effect threshold which define the therapeutic window. In addition, much work has been done in exploring the effects of frequency modulation, which may help patients with gait freezing and other axial symptoms. However, there is a paucity of data on the use of ultra-short pulse width settings which are now possible with technological advances. We also

discuss current evidence for the use of novel programming techniques including directional and adaptive stimulation, and highlight areas for future research.
pubmed.gov https://www.ncbi.nlm.nih.gov/pubmed/28505983

The next few weeks proved to be vitally important. I needed to get as much rest as possible to heal. Very soon we would be turning on the DBS system and calibrating it. During this time, my friend Jean took me in and took excellent care of me. Without her help, I would have been lost. It was during my recovery I had the oddest sensation I have ever felt. While I rested and slept those next two weeks, I could feel my brain repairing itself. It felt almost as though my brain was de-fragging itself like a computer - reorganizing memories, information, and bits of data, in the hard drive of my mind. It felt so strange!

Now, it was time to turn this DBS system on. Dr. Cook's job was completed, surgically installing the batteries, wires, and stimulators. It was now Dr. Abbasi's job to activate, calibrate, and then fine tune the parameters of the DBS system. Dr. Abbasi was responsible for the calibration of all the DBS systems implanted by Dr. Cook. Eagerly, showing up to my scheduled appointment with Dr. Abbasi, I was excited and nervous at the same time. When he first turned on the system, it was set to a minimum setting, allowing time for my brain to get used to the electrical current. Initially, I could hardly feel it. He asked me a few questions to see if I was alright with the settings. I told him I was fine, and he left the room for about twenty minutes or so. When he returned, he got a bit more particular with the region in the brain he wished to stimulate. He determined this by asking me questions as he changed my settings - tweaking and adjusting me through the different settings he would try. While tweaking my settings, he had me walk up and down a hallway to see the effect and results of his changes. Once he made a decision on the region of my brain he found most responsive to the therapy, he added more current incrementally. Again, he asked if I was OK then left for about twenty minutes. This pattern continued for two hours. Each time he changed my settings, he had me walk down the hall to observe my gait. I watched him as he made notations after every series of setting changes, carefully observing my ability to walk. Wouldn't you know it, he was dialing me in. I actually was improving. Amazing! After the two-hour session, Dr. Abbasi thought we had a good base line to move forward with. He told me to live with these settings for a while and call him if I needed him or if any changes needed to be made. Maybe two weeks later, I had one more calibration session with Dr. Abbasi, where he really wanted to drill down and adjust me to the nth degree. Then, off I went!

"Deep brain stimulation," (DBS) is a neurosurgical procedure involving the implantation of a medical device called a neurostimulator (sometimes referred to as a 'brain pacemaker'), which sends electrical impulses, through implanted electrodes, to specific targets in the brain (brain nuclei) for the treatment of movement disorders, including Parkinson's disease, essential tremor, and dystonia.[1] While DBS has proven to be effective for some people, the potential for serious complications and side effects exists. DBS directly changes brain activity in a controlled manner, but its underlying principles and mechanisms are not clear.")
wikipedia.org https://en.wikipedia.org/wiki/Deep_brain_stimulation

I had one final appointment with Dr. Cook. He wanted to check my incisions one last time and see if there were any issues with infection. As Dr. Cook gave my incisions a look see, I asked if there were any physical limitations on what I should, or should not be doing. Dr. Cook's response was succinct and to the point. He said, "Live your life!" I took those words sincerely into my heart, and I thanked him for giving me back my life. I felt an enormous burden had been lifted. The improvement from this operation and all facets of my physical health were immediate and shocking. My gait and walk had been restored to the days when I first took Sinemet. Remarkable! I even felt well enough to play tennis not too long after my surgery. It was simply unbelievable!

While it was true, the DBS operation had rejuvenated my physical being, without question it was also true, the lifestyle problems which had been plaguing me for years, weren't improving at all. My insomnia, which I considered a huge problem and health issue, had not subsided one iota. The odor from my eyes, ears, nose, urine color, and stench was still not good. Also, I hated feeling like I was a slave to the medications. The violent shaking of my body, mostly my legs, never seemed to stop. The daily up-and-down roller coaster ride I had to take with these medications. Working one minute then not working at all the next. The continuing battle with barometric pressure change. It was a daily reminder I still had problems to resolve. Another personal issue I had, two hours before starting each day with a dose of medication, so I could move wasn't how I wanted to live my life. This important part of my postoperative health and lifestyle stayed pretty much the same. There was one critical symptom which was all together halted by implementing this DBS surgery. My seizure-like cramping episodes. They had magically disappeared, which took time for me to see and recognize in myself.

My newfound physical freedom afforded me some time to relax and think about things, intently. I thought back to the years when I did research and control studies for the guitar. I knew from my work in a control studies having two or more variables addressing the same issue results in a false positive, making the test inconclusive. Now I had both the medication and the DBS system addressing the exact same symptoms at the exact same time. I wanted to know what percentage of the medication versus the DBS I was benefiting from - a question I knew no one could answer. After pondering it for a while, I brought it up during a routine appointment with Dr. Abbasi. I asked him flat out what percentage of the DBS system was benefiting me versus the medication. He said, "I really don't know." The very next sentence out of my mouth was, "Doesn't it make sense to take me off the medication completely and calibrate the DBS system without the influence of drugs to see how far I could go without them?" To which Dr. Abbasi said, "We don't do it that way." "Wrong answer," I said. "You're doing it that way for me!" Dr. Abbassi complied, and together the calibration of the DBS system was done without any influences from the medications whatsoever. This was ten months after my initial DBS surgery in August 2008.

Almost immediately after I discontinued the medications, my lifestyle issues began to improve. The first thing I noticed was I stopped shaking, i.e. having dyskinesia. Not a little, mind you. I had miraculously stopped all together, which, was a gigantic relief. Next, I noticed my urine was no longer the dark, burnt-orange color. I wouldn't say it smelled good, but as far as urine goes, the pungent stench seemed to be gone too. Most importantly, my sleep was improving. I was now averaging six to eight hours a night, whereas before I was getting ten to fifteen hours a week. This was a drastic improvement for me and a much- needed change. My eyes, ears, nose, and toxic funky smell cleared up. Over a little time, I realized my issue with barometric pressure changes was related to the medications too because all of a sudden, I stopped being affected by it in the slightest. Somehow I knew improving my physical issues, without addressing my out of balance lifestyle habits brought on by my medications, would prove to be an extremely short-term solution. I needed a lifestyle change which could take me decades down the road not just a solution focusing only on my physical problem, i.e. Parkinson's. I was a young man, only forty-five years old, when I underwent the DBS surgery. My toxicity and acute symptoms due to prolonged use of, Sinemet, Stalevo, and Permax had left me in one hell of a mess. I now realized this new path I was traveling was the best direction for me to take. I felt empowered, by my decision to discontinue my medications, more empowered than I had felt in an exceedingly long time. This was the first step, in a series of better health decisions I would come to make in the next several years. Make no mistake, I firmly believe none of the other decisions I have made would have any hope of success if I continued using the prescribed drug therapy I was on at this time. Nor would my attempt of going off my medications be a possibility without first having the DBS surgery.

Stalevo is an oral drug formulation developed by Novartis that contains a combination of three different drugs — carbidopa, levodopa and entacapone — to treat Parkinson's disease. The three work together to boost the amount of dopamine in the brain, thereby relieving the symptoms of Parkinson's.

parkinsonnewstoday.com https://parkinsonsnewstoday.com/ parkinsons-disease-treatments/non-motor-symptoms/stalevo/

Entacapone, sold under the brand name Comtan among others, is a medication commonly used in combination with other medications for the treatment of Parkinson's disease.[1] Entacapone together with levodopa and carbidopa allows levodopa to have a longer effect in the brain and reduces Parkinson's disease signs and symptoms for a greater length of time than levodopa and carbidopa therapy alone.[1]
Entacapone is a selective and reversible inhibitor of the enzyme catechol-O-methyltransferase (COMT).[1] When taken together with levodopa (L-DOPA) and carbidopa, entacapone stops catechol-O-methyltransferase from breaking down and metabolizing levodopa, resulting in an overall increase of levodopa remaining in the brain and body.[1]
Carbidopa/levodopa/entacapone (Stalevo), a medication developed by Orion Pharma and marketed by Novartis, is a single tablet formulation that contains levodopa, carbidopa, and entacapone.[2]
wikipedia.org https://en.wikipedia.org/wiki/Entacapone

Now, I was looking my disease right in the eyes, and I much preferred it this way! I discovered, I had a new level of control for my health that previously I had given away to the medications. Or this is the way I saw it. What I wasn't aware of at the time I chose to discontinue the medications was just how much they were responsible for some of my debilitating pain. This only became clear to me after I ended my drug use in 2008 and the re calibration session of my DBS with Dr. Abbasi. It is truly important to remember your physicians who don't have Parkinson's disease might understand how to treat the symptoms of the disorder, but they have yet to discover the origin of the disease itself. I can tell you they don't understand what you are feeling, or the personal challenges you may be going through with it. They may empathize, but until someone has the disorder, they can't possibly understand the nature of the struggles involved with being afflicted with such a devastating disease. How could they, really?

As a matter of fact, even today, there is no specific test for diagnosing Parkinson's disease. It tells me the mystery surrounding it has yet to be defined and understood by science. This is why being your own advocate for your health is so vitally important. I encourage anyone and everyone to trust your inner-most feelings regarding your personal health. If something feels wrong to you, don't proceed with it. Then again, if something feels right to you, even if you are the only one who thinks so, I invite you to investigate those feelings and react to them accordingly.

I had decided not to do music any longer. My approach through the years had been, to say the least, out of balance. If I wanted my life to improve, this meant changing my lifestyle. Plus, I wasn't overly convinced I could ever do music without staying up all night. So I preferred not to risk it. In addition, to my improved sleep, I made a commitment to a better diet, cutting out fatty foods, bread, soda, or anything with processed sugar in it. I got serious about the quality of food I was putting in my mouth. I dove into a fruit and vegetable diet with fish and chicken for protein. Eating a ton of salad! I was taking responsibility for what I could do to help improve my lifestyle, I felt empowered and great about my decisions to change.

For many years, I have been a lover of ocean swimming. Part of my exercise routine in the warmer months has been swimming in a little harbor near where I live. I would put on a wetsuit, so I would be positive buoyancy, and I would swim thirty to forty-five minutes. I found this to be rejuvenating in a mental, physical, and spiritual way. No element on earth holds you like water. It quite literally hugs you. While I swam, I felt free from my Parkinson's and more like I was back in my physical body. Back to normal. Most years, I would swim four to five days a week. It was very beneficial to me and still is today.

The next thing I did was buy a used Total Gym off a Craigslist ad for next to nothing. It appeared to be brand new and had only been used apparently as a clothes hamper. Most of my life, I had always maintained myself through participation in sports and working out. These last eight or ten years, it had been quite impossible for me to gain any traction in this area. I started using the Total Gym five to six days a week. It felt amazing to be able to move and workout again. The Total Gym was the perfect tool for a person in my situation. The level of the exercises were easy to adjust. I could calibrate the machine to match my fitness, through resistance. It also helped me to improve my flexibility. For most Parkinson's patients, flexibility can be an issue. It certainly was in my case. I saw the Total Gym as my gateway to physical freedom through better health. My thirtieth class reunion was coming up in a few years, in 2010. I took those next few years to train and get into shape. Using my reunion as the motivation and the payoff for working hard toward my physical goals.

Time passed, and the weight came off. I was feeling much better. I then realized my physical pain had virtually gone away. Zero cramping, headaches, seizures, barometric pressure change, shaking, there was none of it. Now when I wanted to get up in the morning, I just got up. No waiting for medications to kick in. The only troubling thing i.e. symptom, I still had from time to time was I would drop to my knees uncontrollably. But everything else was so drastically improved, I wasn't particularly bothered by it. My commitment to move away from the medications and better sleep, workout, and improve my diet, had remarkable results. It did far more than improve my life. Being off the medications I felt much clearer in my decision-making ability too. While I was on the medications, and I would make plans with friends to do something. There was 65 percent chance, I wouldn't make it. I felt so up and down on the medications. Being off them I was much more even keeled as a person, and it carried over into all aspects of living. Now, I was seeing the old me returning - never late and dependably on time. Someone you could count on. All of these things helped to not only change me physically, but change my opinion of myself internally, thus, offering empowerment and great ammunition for my inner positive voice.

Another wonderful thing which I did for myself in 2008 was take a part-time job at the local golf course as a ranger. It re-engaged me socially, and it was a fun job to have. It suited me much better than staying in a room all by myself, writing and recording music. Being outside with people and in nature is honestly one of the best therapies there is. Most of all, it gave me a new purpose. Next year, will mark my eleventh season working there as a ranger. I absolutely love it!

All of these little changes I made added up to one huge major change in my life. One change leads to another, then another, until finally you're living in a much better place than you ever thought possible. At least, this is how it was in my case. For every significant problem, there waits a wonderful solution. All we need to do is never give up looking for it!

Chapter 6 - Root Rot in The Family Tree

My brother Mark became well versed on the subject of DBS and neurosurgeons around the Boston area. He and I shared similar neurological disorders, but at first our symptoms were different. In the beginning, his affliction was focused more in the area of his neck. Then, like me, his symptoms advanced, increasing in severity and spread to other parts of his body.

Mark was also a patient of Dr. Palmer, where we both sought to find answers to our neurological issues. I was maybe three to four years into my own personal struggle by the time Mark first started showing signs with his neck. He was about 18 years old. Unbelievably, Mark suffered from a rare neurological disorder called spasmodic torticollis, more commonly referred to these days as cervical dystonia. What we didn't know when we were younger was both Mark and I had related forms of dystonia. Mark always referred to me as the sick one in the family. Through the years I watched my brother share my illness in ways I wished I never had to. Mark's symptoms were initially somewhat different from my own. His head would turn uncontrollably to the side at will and stiffen up. Early on he never complained about walking. It was just his neck giving him problems. I never thought for a second our symptoms were so closely related, but they were.

Spasmodic torticollis is an extremely painful chronic neurological movement disorder causing the neck to involuntarily turn to the left, right, upwards, and/or downwards. The condition is also referred to as "cervical dystonia." Both agonist and antagonist muscles contract simultaneously during dystonic movement.[1] Causes of the disorder are predominantly idiopathic. A small number of patients develop the disorder as a result of another disorder or disease. Most patients first experience symptoms midlife. The most common treatment for spasmodic torticollis is the use of botulinum toxin type A.

wikipedia.org https://en.wikipedia.org/wiki/Spasmodic_torticollis

It took Mark a bit longer to show the signs, but he was every bit as ill as I was. As the years passed, I remember looking at my brother's hands. I noticed similar characteristics in their appearance as to my own. The same rigidity, stiffness, and the way they visually appeared. There was no denying our hands showed identical signs that our afflictions might be more closely related than we knew. I would have to have a talk with Dr. Palmer about my observations. Mark had never taken

Sinemet for his cervical dystonia. He was on a different drug therapy program all together. I wondered if my brother could benefit from taking Sinemet. I was in the honeymoon stage with the drug at the time and thought perhaps this could help improve his illness like it had my own. At my next appointment with Dr. Palmer, I told him about my big brother's hands. I told him they looked the same as mine. Dr. Palmer thought a minute and said, "You know, Brian, you're right!" My next question to the doctor was whether Mark could benefit from taking Sinemet. Dr. Palmer smiled and said he just might. He just might. After leaving my appointment with Dr. Palmer, I sped back to Hampton to find Mark and discuss my hypothesis. I was so excited to share this news with him, and was hopeful to see my big brother possibly get some sort of relief.

Not long after, Mark did start taking the drug Sinemet. Then his journey with the medications paralleled my own. Ironically, we both shared the exact same side effects from them. Insomnia, waiting for the medications to kick in, on/off phenomenon i.e. roller coaster, dyskinesia, etc. The only symptom we didn't share was Mark never fell to his knees. He fortunately avoided this one issue all together. When Mark suddenly began to have foot cramps as part of his symptoms, he began to wonder if taking Sinemet was a good idea or not. My brother and

I didn't have the best communication between us back then. So I wasn't aware of his foot cramping. He never shared this part of his plight with me. In retrospect, we both had learned to hide from sharing our pain.

While we both struggled through those years to find a balance with our disease, I watched my brother struggle to find his balance as well. It proved to me how two individuals stricken with such similar disorders can learn to combat their illnesses in such different ways. There is a very fine line between personally fighting a battle with a disease like DRD/PD and fighting yourself. This was a line which I had wrestled with for many years. Watching my brother having to go through the same obstacles I had been through made me feel helpless to ease his pain. Ultimately, the only person's pain I was responsible for easing was obviously my own. This proved to be a large enough challenge for me.

The years went on, so did the progression of our shared diseases. Before I had heard of deep brain stimulation, my big brother was not only aware of it, he had scheduled his DBS surgery in Boston. This news took me by complete surprise, as I was genuinely concerned for him. Mark underwent brain surgery in the quest to find relief to his own painful symptoms. He was scheduled to have a bilateral (DBS) deep brain stimulation operation at Beth Israel Hospital in Boston, Massachusetts. This was one of the choices he made which I could not fathom making. While I had my doubts about the risk versus reward factor, Mark moved forward. Still, I could not believe he had reached this decision as a viable option for his health. It quite literally scared the crap out of me!

The operation and the process on how it would be performed were unique and specialized based upon the surgeon you chose. This procedure for the neurosurgeon was three separate operations in ninety days, allowing time for the body to rest and recover between surgeries. The process broke down implanting the stimulators, batteries, and wires into three operations. This approach was great in theory, horrible in execution. Right away after the first operation, Mark had an infection and started to reject what they had just surgically placed into his body. This resulted in eight corrective surgeries in less than one year. The reality of what my brother's scalp looked like after all of these operations was far worse than any Hollywood made-up Frankenstein monster you could imagine. These doctors in Boston butchered my brother. After more than a year when it was all said and done, he came home still rejecting the implants and still infected. I asked Mark why he put himself at such risk. He said because Lauren, his wife, did not sign up for this. He told me if there were any hope of getting himself back for the both of them, he was going to do it. For the first time in my life, I saw Mark as having a more fearless approach to the disease than I did. This made no sense to me at the time and took me by complete surprise. I have to admit, I saw Mark's decision as probably the bravest thing he could have done for himself in his situation. My brother knew much more than I did about overcoming one's fears. I carefully looked on and would aspire to making Mark's actions my own. I learned from Mark if you don't take any action in your life, you can't expect to get any results. Mark's actions yielded highly unfavorable results, this is for certain. However, he was not yet finished looking for a solution to his medical dilemma. After being home from Boston for a brief period, Mark sought the help of a local neurosurgeon, Dr. Bruce Cook. Dr. Cook's practice was north of Boston and much closer to where we lived in the town of Hampton, New Hampshire. My brother researched Dr. Cook's background and discovered he was also known for performing DBS surgery on Michael J. Fox, which was how Mark came to hear of Dr. Cook in the first place. I could not believe my big brother's guts and fortitude. Working together with Mark, Dr. Cook began to strategize a path back toward better health. Concentrating his efforts on one side of the bilateral mess left by Beth Israel Hospital, Dr. Cook's goal was to stabilize the healthiest side of the implants before attempting to tackle the more difficult side. As I have mentioned on more than one occasion in the book, Beth Israel Hospital was one of those facilities which utilized three separate operations over 90 days, in their approach to DBS surgery. Dr. Cook performed the three different implants, stimulators, wires and batteries in one complete operation. This reduced the risk of infection to Mark by two-thirds. One operation, rather than three. Though it took time for Mark to come back and recover, I watched him as he did. His wife Lauren was right beside him the whole way. With the proper care under Dr. Cook, Mark had zero rejection and infection. My brother showed me true bravery. I feel the point and sentence is worth repeating, "If we take no action in our lives, we can't expect any results." Mark's willingness to try, have a major setback, and keep going had deeply affected me. I had always taken great caution with every decision I had ever made pertaining to my illness, cautiously weighing the risks versus the rewards. When I reached the point and a pain threshold that my life had been so overwhelmingly reduced by my condition, I had Mark's example of strength to help guide the way. Doing nothing but taking the medications became as much a prison as the disease itself. Watching Mark's attempt to improve his condition, regardless the risks, showed me other choices were available which I needed to consider as well. It was through my brother's strength that I found my own. His confidence paved the way for me, as far as DBS goes. And I probably would have never moved forward with the surgery if it were not for Mark.

In 1987, before DBS was a possibility, I made another big life decision, to reconnect with my father. Since my parents' divorce, in 1976, my father had not been a part of our lives on any level. Not a phone call nor a card to check in on us and see how we were. Nothing! He had simply decided to disappear, and disappear he did! It was as if my father had died. Thank god my mother picked up the slack for him. She did everything humanly possible for Mark and me financially and otherwise. She took on the task and responsibility of taking care of both of us, all by herself.

With all of this in the back of my mind, I heard through the grapevine my father was working in Springfield, Massachusetts just a few hours away from where I lived in Hampton. At the time, I was in a relationship with an amazing girl who lived near Springfield in Chicopee, Massachusetts. I knew my Dad worked in proximity to her for about six months. She and I had discussed it, but then it was forgotten. She knew it was a source of great personal pain to me, so she lovingly didn't bring it up at all. I had made no attempts to connect with him up to this point in time. Nor had I shared this information with my brother or mother. All of a sudden, I woke up one morning in Chicopee at her house and announced, "Today's the day." She knew exactly what I meant. After eleven years of no contact at all, I decided one morning to go and see him for the purpose of closure and clearing the air. I had grown tired of all the emotional baggage I had been carrying and needed to figure out how to free myself from it. Christine, my girlfriend, would not let me go alone. I was incredibly nervous and worried about the possible outcome. We arrived at my dad's place of business, and I asked Christine to please wait in the car for me. "I need to do this on my own." As I walked through the door, I was immediately greeted by someone who asked how he could help me. "Is Peter Hall here?" I asked. "Yes, he is. I will get him for you." In just a few short minutes, there he was, my father, magically appearing before my eyes. He held out his hand to greet me, and said, "Hi, I'm Peter Hall." Keeping my hands in my pockets, I said, "I know who you are. Do you know who I am?" As he studied me, I knew he hadn't a clue who I was. He retracted his hand sometime during the awkwardness of the moment. The minutes weighed heavy on us both. I had dark Vuarnet sunglasses on, and I removed them asking, "Do you know who I am, now? He responded, "No, no I don't!" "How does it feel not to know your own son? Tell me how that feels?" I turned around disgusted and made my way to the door to leave. Much to my surprise, my father followed me out asking to speak with me. I sat in his car, talking to him for hours, and I asked him why. For the first time, I saw as much pain in my father's eyes as I had felt in myself for all those years. The answer he gave me made sense and I believed. He said, "The longer I stayed away, the harder it was to come home." Right then and there, I forgave him. I said, "Dad, the fathering days are long gone, but we can form a friendship." He agreed. I cried and told him I loved him and I didn't want him to die alone. We embraced, and both of our lives changed considerably from this point on. Forgiving my father actually freed me in a great many ways. It also taught me an enormous lesson. The key to life is peace. The key to peace is forgiveness. It is impossible to have a peaceful life if you can't offer forgiveness. Forgiving my dad granted me peace to have a better life and helped to heal me inside. However, learning how to forgive myself would be a much more involved and time-consuming process.

This decision to reengage with my father changed the course of everyone's life in my family - my mother, brother, father, and of course, me. The very next day, after I saw him in Springfield, my dad drove to Hampton to see my brother, Mark. Before we knew it, my father moved back to Hampton, where he and my mother reunited. He felt bad about the physical hardships Mark and I were suffering through.

As the years passed, my father's motor function was becoming more and more impaired. Impaired to all of us around him, that's for certain. Dad was slowing down in cognitive thinking, and his ability to walk became noticeably hampered. We all were puzzled by this sudden change in his medical condition. When my father turned 68 years old, he scheduled an appointment with a local neurologist to see what this could be. He was diagnosed with late-onset Parkinson's disease. We all were saddened by the news, but were in no way shocked by this development. It made sense, in a historical family way. At least this was my thinking in processing the news. My father really didn't share his most inner feelings about this diagnosis with me, but I could tell he was scared. As I watched him begin to deteriorate from the symptoms of PD, his life became an example of what I didn't want to emulate. He made no attempts to improve his situation. The neurologist gave him Sinemet at the initial diagnosis to try to improve his symptoms. At first, it seemed to help, but just like Mark and me before him, it didn't help him for too long. His overall condition was a mild case of Parkinson's, his symptoms were nowhere near as acute compared to Mark's or mine. Mark's and my symptoms were much more pronounced and severe. He defiantly refused to do the exercises he was given. His approach to Parkinson's disease was not much of an approach at all. When the disease started to run him over, ill-equipped to combat it, my father without opposition, submitted. Very soon, his lack of initiative came to a head. Then one day, it happened. Dad took a bad fall in the kitchen about the first or second week in November 2008. He fractured his left scapula, (shoulder blade.) To the hospital we went. Dad never walked again. He was so afraid of falling, the fear crippled him, and he didn't take another unassisted step for the rest of his life. He could physically walk, but the fear of falling overwhelmed his ability to try to attempt it. I would stop in at the nursing home for daily visits, hoping to motivate him to participate in the physical therapy. I-asked, "Dad, don't you want to get better and come home?" He said yes, but as far as doing the work, he would have none of it. His condition worsened so quickly. I had never seen anyone decline so fast before. The nursing home where he was being cared for informed us that the local hospice should get involved, and did. He didn't have much time after they were brought in. On the eve of my father's death, I spent the night with him in a private room. The nursing home had moved him into this room for privacy for the family. In four short months after his fall, my father died of a bed sore and complications from Parkinson's disease. But he didn't die alone! My mother, brother, sister-in-law, and I were all there when he passed in early February 2009. He was 72. I remember thinking to myself, was it the disease that took my father's life so quickly? Or rather the way he chose to deal with it? As personal as living is for all of us, I saw right then and there dying is just as personal.

On the opposite end of the personality spectrum, there's my mother. A fiery redheaded Irish lass who doesn't have the tiniest bit of quit in her. Absolutely none! My mother's approach to her life was 180 degrees to that of my father's. She has struggled and fought her entire existence with Crohn's disease, never giving in or giving up to her illness. Mom has lived in the face of pain for so long, and nothing keeps her down. Since the age of 17, she has battled so hard just to keep on living. As a matter of fact, when she was 20, one doctor gave her a year to live. Undeterred by anything which happens to get in her way, Mom is still going strong. As of October 2019, she is now 88 years old. Her example and zeal for life are to be commended, and have always impressed me. I have never heard her complain, or make excuses. She is committed to getting on with living and has always been this way. Here's a woman who has been sick her whole life, while my father had been healthy for his, except the last four years. The only thing I can think of is maintaining a healthy outlook and attitude. I would imagine it has more of an impact on our overall health than we can even know. It would be so nice to think perhaps I inherited some of the strength my mom possesses. And, I suppose I must have, because nothing much ever gets me down.

Crohn's disease is a type of inflammatory bowel disease (IBD) that may affect any part of the gastrointestinal tract from mouth to anus.[2] Signs and symptoms often include abdominal pain, diarrhea (which may be bloody if inflammation is severe), fever, and weight loss.[1][2] Other complications may occur outside the gastrointestinal tract and include anemia, skin rashes, arthritis, inflammation of the eye, and tiredness.[1] The skin rashes may be due to infections as well as pyoderma gangrenosum or erythema nodosum.[1] Bowel obstruction may occur as a complication of chronic inflammation, and those with the disease are at greater risk of bowel cancer.[1]

While the cause of Crohn's disease is unknown, it is believed to be due to a combination of environmental, immune, and bacterial factors in genetically susceptible individuals.[6][7][8] It results in a chronic inflammatory disorder, in which the body's immune system attacks the gastrointestinal tract possibly directed at microbial antigens.[7][9] While Crohn's is an immune-related disease, it does not appear to be an autoimmune disease (in that the immune system is not being triggered by the body itself).[10] The exact underlying immune problem is not clear; however, it may be an immunodeficiency state.[9][11][12] About half of the overall risk is related to genetics with more than 70 genes having been found to be involved.[1][13] Tobacco smokers are twice as likely to develop Crohn's disease as nonsmokers.[3] It also often begins after gastroenteritis.[1] Diagnosis is based on a number of findings including biopsy and appearance of the bowel wall, medical imaging and description of the disease.[1] Other conditions that can present similarly include irritable bowel syndrome and Behçet's disease.[1] There are no medications or surgical procedures that can cure Crohn's disease.

<u>wikipedia.org https://en.wikipedia.org/wiki/Crohn%27s_disease</u>

My mother and I have spoken at great length about Mark's PD and my own. She expressed concern and wondered while carrying us both whether Mark and I got enough nutrition from her. I'm sure this is a possibility and something to medically consider. Another possibility - she told me when she gave birth to us, but particularly me, she was deathly ill during childbirth. Subsequently, so was I. I barely survived! When the doctor delivered me, the umbilical cord was wrapped around my neck, or, so she told me. I know my mother carries guilt about having two sons stricken with this devastating disease. However, it is no one's fault. This is the hand we were dealt in life. The best we can do is get on with it, and play the cards we have.

At the age of 6 years old, well into my 40s, I had severe stomach aches and stomach cramps, i.e. constipation. I would sit in pain for hours on the toilet. As a kid, the pain was excruciating. It was so bad, in fact, mom would have to come into the bathroom and rub my belly in a gentle, circular motion to ease my pain. I recall numerous times a month having constipation like this. My mother would confide in me, saying, "I pray to God you don't have Crohn's disease. I pray you don't." I don't remember my brother ever having gut issues as a precursor symptom to Parkinson's disease. Regardless, I found it odd we didn't share this characteristic.

The medical community now says one of the first symptoms of Parkinson's disease can be constipation. And, boy, this was certainly the case, in my situation when I was a youngster. I still remember the horrible taste of the mineral oil my mom gave me to clear the blockage.

The stuff tasted gross and was terrible to take. What I found enormously helpful with my constipation has been a healthy diet. Later in life, I started to eat organic, and it has cleared up those gut issues of mine completely.

Six or eight years ago, I was invited to a lecture given by Dr. William Servert, from Beth Israel Medical Center in New York City. He traveled all the way to Portsmouth, New Hampshire to speak on the subject of Parkinson's disease. It seemed like a wonderful opportunity to learn something new, and it was. The man was a truly knowledgeable neurologist and had an abundance of information. He was the first neurologist I ever heard say, "The belly is the second brain," and that gut health is something to consider with Parkinson's disease. He also mentioned it was too early on in the research to commit to anything, but he thought that this connection would prove to be vitally important in unlocking the mysteries of Parkinson's disease. I could see a healthy diet must play a gigantic role in our gut health. This was another big reason why I started caring so much, about what I put in my mouth for nutrition.

Parkinson's disease, which involves the malfunction and death of nerve cells in the brain, may originate in the gut, new research suggests, adding to a growing body of evidence supporting the idea.
The new study shows that a protein in nerve cells that becomes corrupted and then forms clumps in the brains of people with Parkinson's can also be found in cells that line the small intestine. The research was done in both mice and human cells. The finding supports

the idea that this protein first becomes altered in the gut and then travels to the brain, where it causes the symptoms of Parkinson's disease.

Parkinson's disease is a progressive movement disorder, affecting as many as 1 million people in the United States and 7 million to 10 million people worldwide, according to the Parkinson's Disease Foundation. The protein, called alpha-synuclein, is abundant in the brain. And in healthy nerve cells, it dissolves in the fluid within the cell. But in Parkinson's patients, alpha-synuclein folds abnormally. The misfolded protein can then spread through the nervous system to the brain as a prion, or infectious protein. In the brain, the misfolded protein molecules stick to each other and clump up, damaging neurons. [6 Foods That Are Good for Your Brain] In 2005, researchers reported that people with Parkinson's disease who had these clumps in their brains also had the clumps in their guts. Other research published this year looked at people who had ulcers and who underwent a surgery that removed the base of the vagus nerve, which connects the brain stem to the abdomen. These patients had a 40 percent lower risk of developing Parkinson's later in life compared with people who didn't have their vagus nerve removed. Both findings suggested the prion may originate in the gut. But one puzzle remained: how the proteins that became altered in the gut could spread to the brain. The protein had been found in the lumen, or the space inside the gastrointestinal tract, but "nerves are not open to the lumen," said gastroenterologist Dr. Rodger Liddle, senior author of the new paper, appearing today (June 15) in the journal JCI Insight, and professor of medicine at Duke University in North Carolina. A key clue to how the protein may move from the lumen into nerve cells came in 2015. Liddle's team discovered cells in the lining of the small intestine that "acted a lot like nerve cells," Liddle said. The cells were endocrine cells, meaning they produce hormones, but they contained neurotransmitters and other proteins normally found in neurons. These cells even appeared to branch out in a similar way that neurons do, to communicate.

When placed near neurons, these endocrine cells behaved a lot like neurons – the endocrine cells moved toward the neurons, and fibers sprouted between the cells, connecting them, Liddle said. The process was captured in a time-lapse video featured in the 2015 study in the Journal of Clinical Investigation.

101

"It was only afterwards that we started putting these things together — these cells have a lot of nerve-like properties, [so] let's see if they also contain alpha-synuclein. And if they do, maybe they could be the source of Parkinson's disease," Liddle told Live Science. [10 Things You Didn't Know About the Brain] Now that Liddle's team has shown that the endocrine cells do, in fact, contain the alpha-synuclein protein, the researchers want to establish that the endocrine cells of Parkinson's patients carry the malformed version of the protein, Liddle said. If they can establish that, Liddle said, they can envision how the corrupted proteins causing Parkinson's disease could spread from the gut lining to the brain, possibly via the vagus nerve. Previous research has shown that people exposed to certain pesticides and bacteria are more likely to get Parkinson's. Liddle said that one possibility is that these agents may affect the nerve-like endocrine cells in the gut, altering the structure of the alpha-synuclein protein inside the gut cells. "Maybe it's bacteria, maybe a toxin that people ingest. Maybe they affect the endocrine cell and that corrupts the alpha-synuclein protein, and that spreads from the cell to the vagus nerve to the brain," Liddle told Live Science. For now, many "maybe's" remain. But if further research supports the hypothesis, it could point the way to new ways to diagnose Parkinson's disease early on, as well as to new approaches to treatment, Liddle said. "It's possible that if it starts in the gut, then you could create treatments that prevent abnormal alpha-synuclein formation in these cells," Liddle said. "It's possible you could develop dietary ways of treating those cells because those cells are lining the intestine. At this point, it's difficult to imagine, but we will see."

livescience.com https://www.livescience.com/59498-parkinsons-disease-may-begin-in-gut.html

I have found this information beneficial to me in the way I have chosen to combat my Parkinson's. Instead of taking medications, I learned by eating only organic and whole foods, also seeking out non-GMO verified food products, has greatly improved my gut health and overall health. It is a noticeable difference which I can see in my day-to-day life and health. This approach really was working for me. Rather than taking pills, improved sleep, better diet and a regimented exercise program proved to be a much more stable approach in the taming of my disorder for my particular situation.

Undeniably, it would seem in my family, genetics had loaded the gun, and the environment pulled the trigger. Meaning, every male member was neurologically impacted by Parkinson's disease in only two short generations in my family. No history of neurodegenerative disease has ever showed up in our family tree before. So, could this be only genetics? Or the combination of a genetic predisposition to the Parkinson's gene brought on by environmental chemical exposure? In my lifetime, I may never discover the real truth.

Chapter 7 - Once You Learn ~

As much as I would like to take full credit for my brilliant new diet strategy, I really can't. A wonderful woman named Brenda made that happen. She brought organic food into my life and a non-GMO way of thinking. We met in September 2011, and I fell head over heels for her. Having Parkinson's disease, falling head over heels in front of anyone wasn't all that unusual or special, to be frank. But seriously, soon after we met, Brenda and I became a couple. She was a woman of many passions and talents. Brenda's career path brought her into the world of nursing. Actually, she was an exceptionally committed and insightful maternity nurse., Her ability to see medical issues in her infant patients, helped her to excel in her career. This medical foresight she possesses, became the voice for children that could not speak themselves. Resulting in Brenda being responsible for saving many new infants lives. Being much more knowledgeable than myself about diet and the chemicals found in food these days, she helped to educate me. She brought me up to speed on the do's and don'ts of eating a healthy diet. Taking a real caring interest in me and my health. It seemed she wanted to know the origin of my disorder as much as I did. Brenda believed perhaps chemicals in the food I had eaten might have triggered Parkinson's in both me and Mark. I don't know. I suppose anything is possible.

My new approach to food now became a simple one. I had a big-time, full-blown sugar addiction. Cakes, pies, ice cream, cookies, those sorts of sugary treats. To break the cycle of those go-to food items I was so addicted to, I replaced them and my cravings for sugar with organic fruit like apples, oranges, bananas, etc. Eliminating breads and grains seemed to help me as well. I started drinking a smoothie every day for breakfast and I began to feel so much better. This new diet strategy coupled with my exercise program and improved sleep from being off the medications for Parkinson's, added up to a gigantic lifestyle change. The more I learned from Brenda what was in the food we all ate, the more concerned I became about it in my own life. There is a great deal of new information linking GMOs to Parkinson's disease and other neurodegenerative disorders. Here is some good information to read up on GMOs.

oradix.com https://oradix.com/parkinson-s-disease-caused-by-glyphosate-monsanto-and-or-trichloroethylene/

huffpost.com https://www.huffpost.com/entry/parkinsons-and-produce_b_4312315

https://www.creators.com/read/c-force/05/13/pesticides-parkinsons-gmos-and-your-food-part-1

Another excellent resource on the subject of organic food and GMOs is Jeffrey Smith, at IRT, the Institute for Responsible Technology. I have found no one more knowledgeable than Mr. Smith on the subject of GMOs in our food supply. For many years he has worked tirelessly, to educate people all over the globe about the dangers of GMOs in our food supply. I encourage you to look him up. He is easy to find on the internet.

What is a GMO?
Genetically modified organisms (GMOs) are living organisms whose genetic material has been artificially manipulated in a laboratory through genetic engineering. This creates combinations of plant, animal, bacteria, and virus genes that do not occur in nature or through traditional crossbreeding methods.

Most GMOs have been engineered to withstand the direct application of herbicide and/or to produce an insecticide. However, new technologies are now being used to artificially develop other traits in plants, such as a resistance to browning in apples, and to create new organisms using synthetic biology. Despite biotech industry promises, there is no evidence that any of the GMOs currently on the market offer increased yield, drought tolerance, enhanced nutrition, or any other consumer benefit.

Visit the <u>What is GMO</u> page for more information and a list of high-risk crops.

Are GMOs safe?

In the absence of credible independent long-term feeding studies, the safety of GMOs is unknown. Increasingly, citizens are taking matters into their own hands and choosing to opt out of the GMO experiment.

Are GMOs labeled?

Sixty-four countries around the world, including Australia, Japan, and all of the countries in the European Union, require genetically modified foods to be labeled. <u>1</u> While a 2015 ABC News survey found that 93% of Americans believe genetically modified foods should be labeled, GMOs are not required to be labeled in the U.S. and Canada. <u>2</u> In the absence of mandatory labeling, the Non-GMO Project was created to give consumers the informed choice they deserve.

Which foods might contain GMOs?

Most packaged foods contain ingredients derived from corn, soy, canola, and sugar beet — and the vast majority of those crops grown in North America are genetically modified. <u>3</u>

To see a list of high-risk crops, visit the <u>What is GMO</u> page.

Animal products: The Non-GMO Project also considers livestock, apiculture, and aquaculture products at high risk because genetically engineered ingredients are common in animal feed. This impacts animal products such as: eggs, milk, meat, honey, and seafood.

Processed inputs, including those from synthetic biology: GMOs also sneak into food in the form of processed crop derivatives and inputs derived from other forms of genetic engineering, such as synthetic biology. Some examples include: hydrolyzed vegetable protein corn syrup, molasses, sucrose, textured vegetable protein, flavorings, vitamins yeast products, microbes & enzymes, flavors, oils & fats, proteins, and sweeteners.

How do GMOs affect farmers?

Because GMOs are novel life forms, biotechnology companies have been able to obtain patents to control the use and distribution of their genetically engineered seeds. As a result, the companies that make GMOs now have the power to sue farmers whose fields have been contaminated with GMOs, even when it is the result of the drift of pollen from neighboring fields.<u>4</u>

Genetically modified crops therefore pose a serious threat to farmer sovereignty and to the national food security of any country where they are grown.

What are the impacts of GMOs on the environment?

More than 80% of all genetically modified crops grown worldwide have been engineered for herbicide tolerance.5 As a result, the use of toxic herbicides, such as Roundup®, has increased fifteenfold since GMOs were first introduced.6 In March 2015, the World Health Organization determined that the herbicide glyphosate (the key ingredient in Roundup®) is "probably carcinogenic to humans."

Genetically modified crops also are responsible for the emergence of "superweeds" and "superbugs," which can only be killed with ever more toxic poisons such as 2,4-D (a major ingredient in Agent Orange). 7,8

Most GMOs are a direct extension of chemical agriculture and are developed and sold by the world's largest chemical companies. The longterm impacts of these GMOs are unknown. Once released into the environment, these novel organisms cannot be recalled.

nongmoproject.org https://www.nongmoproject.org/gmo-facts/

I found this information critical in reaching another level in my quest to be a healthier person. The more time elapsed, I could see and feel this investment was paying me huge dividends. It may not have been apparent to the outside world, but it became apparent to me internally. The better I felt, the more empowered and committed I became. I gained slight confidences all along the way. However, the topic of organic foods and GMOs can be a confusing subject to wrap your head around. In my case, I just broke it down and made it as easy as possible, by eating strictly organic whole fruits, vegetables, and organic free-range meats. If you are a meat eater, it can also be somewhat tricky to navigate. The factory farming of beef, pork, poultry including eggs, and even fish like salmon in the United States might be fed with man-made grains containing GMOs. Free-range organically fed birds and wild-caught fish are the healthiest solutions to avoid GMOs in your diet. Also, I would look for local grass-fed beef, again avoiding the grain-fed beef containing GMOs. If I was not sure about the meat and its content, I wouldn't buy it. Our food supply is frighteningly compromised with chemicals and other hazardous things most of us are not even aware of. I found it best to arm myself with knowledge and stay apprised regarding the information on the subject of organics and GMO foods. Through Brenda's help and guidance, 1 learned what to eat and more importantly, what not to eat. The results were those healthier choices became a new platform for me taking back some control in my life for my own health.

There were still so many things I wasn't able to do, during those days. For instance, I couldn't walk well. I couldn't run or jog. Basically, I couldn't move freely through the world, as we know it. As limiting as I found my situation, I always felt fortunate. I had many friends and family who I loved and who loved me the way I was. I took it as a true blessing. While it was true I had DBS and had discontinued my medications for more than four years, I felt better this way than I had ever felt dealing with my disease at any other time since my symptoms first appeared. Outside looking in, though, told a much different story. I am sure to the world, I must appear like a land flounder. And that is fine. I had long since grown out of being concerned about how I appeared on the outside. I was devoted and committed to feeling better on the inside. Quite a change for me to make, but somehow I made it.

One of the most interesting things about Parkinson's disease is this disease is always on the move. When you think you have a handle on it, it throws you the most god-awful breaking ball to try to hit. From my experience I have learned what works today and grants you relief from your symptoms may not work tomorrow. The disease is constantly changing, evolving, and progressing. So our approach to combating our illness has to be forever evolving and changing too. At first, the medications gave me miraculous results. Those effects didn't seem to last long. The DBS has had a similar pattern. However, the DBS without medications has been a much more stable way to combat my symptoms. The highs aren't as high, but the lows are nowhere near as low. Being prepared for the next solution and always on the lookout to try new things to better your health, I have found to be most valuable. Admittedly, my experience with Parkinson's disease has always been a reactive relationship, reacting to the symptoms I am feeling due to the disease at any given time. My dream is to one day have a proactive approach to this disorder for everyone!

In the summer of 2013, Brenda and I were living together. We had just moved into a nice apartment in Exeter, New Hampshire, leaving the winter rental we had at the beach. You might be thinking to yourself, "Exeter, again Brian?" And, I agree. When I was younger, Exeter's appeal and charm was wasted on me. I was ecstatic to be moving in there with Brenda. It was a lovely place to live. One beautiful Sunday, Brenda announced to me, "Brian, I want to go and get a mountain bike today." I smiled and said, "OK." There was a bike store just about five-hundred yards from our place. I asked her, "Would you like me to come with you?" "Oh sure," Brenda said. And off we went. We parked the car in the handicap space, and Brenda sauntered right in the bike store. I followed her in, like a fish out of water, flopping all over the place like I always did. I looked on with anticipation as she tried out different bicycle models. She rode a few of them outside, around the store, and then she chose one. All of a sudden, it hit me. I turned to her and said, "Hey, Bren, wouldn't it be really something if I got a bike too, and we could share mountain biking together?" Her smile and joy left her face. She said to me, "No flipping way you're getting a bicycle." I understood why she reacted that way. After all, I could barely walk in the bike store. How the heck could I ride a bicycle? My answer is, you don't know until you try. The outside world's view of what I was capable of was in no way aligned with my own views of myself. That's for sure!

My walking by this time had gotten to be mentally taxing on me. The focus and concentration it took to get from point A to point B was exhausting. A staggering amount of nuances, ran through my head at the same time. Balance, gait, picking my feet up, alternating my arm swing. None of this came naturally or without thought. Whenever I needed to move, I was bogged down with these worrisome thoughts.

Brenda's negative response to my getting a bicycle I thought was due mostly to fear and worry. Worry about my falling and injuring myself, which was reasonable and made good sense. Unfortunately, for Brenda, I didn't and don't subscribe to that sort of thinking. The very next day, Monday while she was at work, I went to the same bike shop. I spoke to the owner at length about having Parkinson's disease and the enormous length of time it had been since I had even ridden a bike. It had to be close to thirty-five years, or more. He said, "Well let's get you on one, and we shall see, right?" I must admit, I was a bit nervous. More nervous about totaling the bike and having to buy it than hurting myself. Together, the owner of the bike shop and I picked out a model in my size. We made our way outside, so I could try it out. As he steadied the bike, I struggled to get my right leg over the seat. I have to say, the hardest part of the entire experience was getting on and off the bike. Flexibility in my legs is exceedingly limited. In a word poor! He looked me over and made a few adjustments with the seat and handlebars, taking into account my inflexibility. "I think you are all set to go, Brian," he said. Placing my right foot on the pedal and pushing forward with my left foot on the ground, I started riding. I rode around the building a few times, gaining confidence with every lap. The owner, John, could not believe his eyes. I was pretty surprised myself, but elated with the outcome. I asked the owner, "Before I buy this bike, and I am buying this bike, would you call my girlfriend, Brenda, and tell her what you witnessed here today. She wasn't supportive in me getting a bicycle. I don't want to worry the poor woman to death." He said, "Gladly! "By the way, Brian, you ride this bike far better than you walk."

Brenda received John's voice mail. Sadly, her skepticism would take more time to dissolve. Her concerns and worries about me riding a bicycle ran far deeper than I initially realized. We started taking short rides through the woods together. Nothing too technical as far as terrain or mountain bike riding was concerned, but riding nonetheless. There was a feeling of physical freedom that came over me while on a bike I hadn't felt in many years. The feeling was similar to skiing. Riding through the woods in nature, I felt like I was physically reborn. This is the best way to describe the feeling riding gives me. Taking some rides on my own was a real sense of freedom. The more time passed, the more challenging the rides became, either in distance or terrain. It wasn't long before Brenda finally admitted to me I was a stronger rider than she was. Though her concerns were not completely gone yet, it was an activity we both enjoyed sharing together.

I had been an avid golfer for many years. One might have surmised this already since I'm a ranger at a golf course. The trouble all started with golf when the falling to my knees phenomenon began years earlier. In fact, I would fall uncontrollably on the greens, leaving behind impressions on the greens from my knees. I felt so bad about damaging the golf course, I decided to give up the game. Everyone who plays golf understands that is what you are paying for when you buy your ticket to play. "Greens fees." All golf courses spend an exorbitant amount of time and money keeping the greens in shape. I just couldn't feel good about playing golf any longer, damaging courses. So I listed my golf clubs on Craigslist, along with the new bike I just bought. They both sold right away, and I bought myself a full suspension enduro mountain bike. Used of course! The first bike I purchased was a beginner hardtail mountain bike. This new bike would take me deeper and further into the sport than the other mountain bike ever could.

Not too long after this, I became aware our landlord of our new apartment in Exeter was an accomplished mountain bike rider. When I told him I had just purchased a full suspension mountain bike, we instantly connected and aligned on the subject. It gave us something we could bond over and build a friendship upon. Now it was obvious and apparent to us both, we shared a passion for mountain bike riding. He said, "We need to get together and do a ride, sometime." I agreed. In a short time, we did exactly that. We made plans to ride together at Stratham Hill Park. Stratham Hill Park, just the title alone gives you the picture the terrain might be something other than flat. It was more hilly than I was used to. It also had more technical features. Bridges, rock walls, and somewhat extreme gnarly terrain were all on the menu at Stratham Hill. It definitely was a step up in my technical riding of a level or two.

Steve my landlord, is a very matter-of-fact type of person. He doesn't sugar coat things or give people a story. He is a straight shooter. If you can't deal with hearing the truth, you shouldn't deal with Steve. This is one of the qualities I appreciate most about Steve's personality, and to be honest, the reason why I love the guy! He treated me like any other able-bodied rider. No different from anyone else, which was just the way I wanted it!

At Stratham Hill, the terrain was far more treacherous than any I had ridden on before. It really didn't concern me, though. Steve and I met at the park on a fall day for our first ride together. I was so excited to experience this new level of riding and to have a friend to share the experience with. Steve took me on an easy trail, but when we came to cross the first plank bridge, I reared up like a horse and wiped out, ending up in the muddy brook. It was dry that day, thank goodness. However, it did not slow me down for long. Mountain biking is a sport that graciously accepts participants who fall. My outlook was and still is, if you're not falling, you're not testing yourself or your skills as a mountain bike rider. So this made me feel right at home! Unembarrassed, I got up, brushed myself off, and Steve and I had a bit of a laugh over my unscheduled dismount. Steve told me, "Keep your head up going over those narrow bridges, Brian, and you'll be fine." The next challenge was keeping up with Steve on the steeper long hill climbs. I found this to be the hardest part of the ride. Going up the inclines of any significance, I would invariably stall my bike out by picking a bad line or hitting a protruding root or rock with my front tire. This was sapping my strength because once I stopped, I could no longer get back in the saddle and continue. I was unable to walk with the bike, up or down the trail. So the best solution I found was to get the bicycle turned around and head back down the way I came. My newfound freedom was beginning to feel just like skiing with your kids. Guess who the kid was in this scenario? You got it. Me!

After Steve introduced me to the park, I went there to ride on my own. I would spend hours practicing going over the plank bridges and ride the trails wherever I could. I was frustrated by the limitations placed on my freedom by the trails with imposing hills. Attempting to ride up them, but I always came off the saddle, killing my momentum to reach to top. In between rides, I would watch YouTube videos on mountain biking techniques and positioning. Anything I could do to learn more and improve as a rider, that's what I did. About three weeks later, Steve and I scheduled another ride at Stratham Hill Park. Mounting our bikes, we both set off. Steve noticed right away my riding had improved, and said, "Wow, you look like you have been practicing. Big improvement, Brian, big improvement." However, when we reached the hilly section of the park, I was faced with the same results

- coming out of the saddle due to stalling. I noticed Steve's bike seat went up and down. When I asked him about his unique seat, he explained to me a "dropper seat post," can be raised or lowered, depending on the terrain you are riding on. He said, "Most riders set it at the lowest position for hill descents, thus, enabling the rider to lower his center of gravity. You would have the best results keeping it at the normal ride position, the rest of the time," he went on to say. It sounded like a huge technical advantage to me, so I went online to research dropper seat posts. I saw there was a button installed on the handlebars to raise or lower the seat post. So simple and easy! What I also learned was they were as much as an advantage as I thought, but much more expensive than I could afford - about half the price of my entire bike. The next week, I found a box on our front porch. I brought the box inside and opened it. Unbelievably, it was a new dropper seat post. I noticed a note from Steve stating to use this in good health. He thought it might help me stay on the bike when I stalled out going up hills. Steve had upgraded his dropper seat post and gave me his older one. Not wasting a moment, I installed it right away and went for a ride. For a non-able-bodied rider, the advantages to having this piece of equipment are immeasurable. It makes mounting and dismounting my bike much easier. And when I stall out on a hill climb, I can lower my seat before I stall and not come off my bike.

A huge advantage for someone in my situation. No matter what I did, though, hills were a big obstacle that I would need to figure out how to get around.

Like anything, the more time I spent riding my bike, the better I became at it. Once I had ridden a new trail a few times, I could memorize the terrain and get more comfortable riding it. The first time I rode unfamiliar terrain, the outcome was not so good. I would inevitably choose bad lines and tend to crash my bike, making a mess of it, similar to when I walked. The anxiety of not knowing what was ahead of me would get in my head, the nerves and indecision taking over. Then crash! This was not a new development for me, not at all.

I have no idea what the connection might be, how a Parkinson's patient can pedal a bike with any success, but not be able to walk. It amazes me how those two different skill sets don't translate to each other. With me, they certainly don't. All I can tell you in my world, walking creates stress, while riding a bike creates freedom. If I decided to ride a road bicycle, where rocks, massive roots, stone walls, and plank bridges were not obstacles a rider would have to contend with, I would never come off my bike or out of the saddle. These days, I feel there are too many distracted drivers on the roads. So I feel much safer and at home in the woods. There are many examples of Parkinson's patients riding a bicycle on the internet. One of my favorites is "Ride With Larry." It is a documentary on the life of Larry Smith, a man living with Parkinson's disease. He rode a three-wheeled, tadpole trike three-hundred miles across the state of South Dakota. I found some of my motivation to start riding a bike, after I watched Larry's movie. Larry's story and grit inspired me and helped me see the possibilities are endless, as long as we believe in them. I highly recommend you watch the documentary" Ride With Larry." I bet you, too, will be inspired.

Hope and inspiration are vitally important to maintain in everyone's life. These qualities are around us and in us too. All we have to do is tap into them. Recently, I watched as a close high school friend was diagnosed with Parkinson's disease. The news of his diagnosis devastated both him and his family. Michael loves the White Mountains, cross-country skiing, and hiking through the White Mountain National Forest. An avid outdoorsman, he is. Michael and I have had long philosophical discussions regarding Parkinson's and the physical changes he soon would be experiencing. He was scared, of course, but I tried to reassure him he would be OK. I also shared with him there are a number of phases every Parkinson's patient sooner or later goes through. Anger, sadness, or depression, then hopefully acceptance.

One of the most difficult phases I mentioned to him was mourning the loss of your physical person. Which, happens to be a common response to being initially diagnosed with Parkinson's! I shared this with Michael and watched as he made adjustments to living his life. When he would stumble, he picked himself right back up again, always being a positive guy. Michael's symptoms were much different from my own. His arms and hands were affected the most. Like my legs and feet, his arms and hands were stiff and rigid. This caused Michael great difficulty in feeding himself or any such routines that required dexterity and coordination with his upper extremities. I also mentioned to him Parkinson's does take a great deal from you, but it gives back too. I am not sure if Michael understood what I meant, but I hoped in time he would. Parkinson's helped me to focus on what was truly important to me, giving me a part of myself I never knew existed. I also shared with him he should not give up on his physical goals and dreams. Today, Michael is actively involved in the Rock Steady Boxing Program for Parkinson's patients, and he has become a certified Rock Steady coach and mentor. Besides his noted accomplishments, he recently embarked on a hiking trip with his wife, Michele, to Switzerland, exploring the Alps. My friend Michael and many others show me every day that Parkinson's disease is not the end. It's a new beginning. I watched as Parkinson's help my friend grow in ways that paralleled my own experiences living with the disorder. Recognizing a self-acceptance and self-love in him now, I had not seen before. Michael has developed a strength through wrestling with Parkinson's disease, I doubt he would have uncovered in himself otherwise. At least, this is what I see and feel about the subject.

Chapter 8 - Aim High ~ Dream Big

During our years together, Brenda and I took many excursions to the Mount Washington Valley. Both of us enjoyed the solitude and laid back nature of the people. From summer kayaking trips down the Saco River, to wonderful snowmobile tours through the White Mountain National Forest - we loved it up there. It was on one of those winter trips while visiting friends in Berlin, New Hampshire when it suddenly struck me. For quite some time, Brenda had suggested to me I write a book, and she would support me in this goal. While her suggestion had planted the seed to get the book started, unfortunately a good working title for the project had eluded me. During our weekend together in Berlin, the title for this book came to me. I also jotted down some ideas for chapter titles in my phone the same weekend. Thus, the humble beginnings of this book project were born.

While driving back down the valley from Berlin, Brenda and I made a stop on the side of the road. The day was a perfect, vivid blue sky winter day. Bitter cold, with glistening snow as far as you could see. We stopped at a valley pass where we could see Mount Washington through this breathtaking river gorge. The snow was so incredibly high from the snow plows. We both climbed up the gigantic snow embankment to get a better view of Mount Washington. Reaching the top, we both sunk in the snow right up to our waists. Laughing, I shouted up to Mount Washington, "My name is Brian Hall, and I am not afraid to fall." The air was so still at that moment, with the dense blanket of snow, I could hear the echo of my own voice reverberating through the pass. We fought to break free from being stuck in waste deep powder and begrudgingly made our way back to the car, both covered in white. It was a moment I shall never forget.

Bren and I continued driving down to Jackson, New Hampshire, when on the way we passed the Mount Washington Auto Road. I thought to myself how wonderful it would be to have an opportunity to do some sort of physical challenge, like riding a bike up the Mount Washington Auto Road. It would most assuredly pose a physical and mental challenge to prepare for. Someday, maybe someday.

Time went by, and I continued to grow my skills slowly as a mountain biker. I saw overall improvement in my riding. However, no matter what I seemed to do to train on hillclimbs, I was not improving in this category at all. A friend had mentioned to me the geometry of my mountain bike, being a 2003 model could be the culprit. Bikes have taken enormous strides in technology since that time he said. I imagined he was correct. The next obvious question was, is there another bike that might work better for my particular needs. The search was on.

I began to demo different mountain bike models, with some limited success. The new bike geometry was a substantial improvement and noticeable. While I felt some difference, being a non-abled-bodied rider, the difference I felt was not worth the price tags of these mountain bikes. At least, not for me. So, I decided to wait a little longer. Then the pedal assist E bikes hit the market. This was the technology I had been waiting for. Pedal assist E bikes are not to be confused with other E bikes utilizing a throttle to propel the bicycle forward. Pedal assist E bikes strictly uses the rider's own pedal stroke energy, thus augmenting your own energy into electricity. These pedal assist E bikes have a few different modes to determine the amount of assist, or energy you may need or desire while out on the trail. Pedal assist E bikes will only move if you pedal.

They are most similar to bicycles. Throttle assist E bikes are most similar to a motor bike.

My local bike store allowed me to demo one of these amazing bikes at the Stratham Hill Park. A place I knew well. I also knew all the trails which were inaccessible to me on a regular mountain bicycle. These new pedal assist E bikes are much heavier than a regular mountain bike, due to the battery and the motor mounted at the cranks, i.e. pedals. But man, once I was on and riding, it was unlike anything I had ever ridden before. For the first test of my demo, I would attempt to go up to the top of Stratham Hill, making it to the fire towers - something I had only done one time without coming out of the saddle, in countless attempts. This trail has a serious pitch to it and an extreme steep grade in places. When I pedaled past the place on the trail where I normally would come off my bike, I could not believe it! I made it up the entire run without an issue. Shocked in disbelief, I zoomed back down the trail to try it again, with even better results the second time. I continued to make my way around Stratham Hill Park, to ride parts of it I had never fully experienced before. Every hill I encountered, every riding challenge that came my way, I could do it. This new pedal assist E bike was an immediate game changer. As far as I was concerned, there was just no way I wouldn't find myself owning one of these life-changing pedal assist E bikes.

Returning to the bike store, caked and covered in mud from head to toe, I was sporting the biggest smile I had worn in some time. The guys at the shop were all eager to hear my review of the bike's performance. When I told them the results of my ride were nothing short of miraculous, they knew they had made a sale. I placed my order for a pedal assist E mountain bike, right then and there.

One of my best friends – Peter - I made aware of this extremely cool pedal assist E bike I had discovered and told him of my new bike purchase. I expressed to him just how much freedom it provided to me as a mountain bike rider. Excited to hear my news, and probably a bit concerned as well, Peter bought a new mountain bike for himself soon after, so we could start riding together - sparing me the worry of riding alone and perhaps his worry too.

When our bicycles came in, Peter and I met at Stratham Hill Park for the maiden voyage and christening of our new toys. Peter had extensive road cycling experience but little to no mountain biking seat time. We donned our helmets and other biking garb. It was a perfect day for a bike ride. Sunny, warm but the park was a little wet in spots, due to a few weeks of rain. No matter, I was pumped for this. I led as Peter followed. Up hills, down hills, through fields, over bridges, including on single-track trails. We did it all! It was on one of these single-track trails, where I had an unforgettable experience. I was coming around the single-track run, deep in the woods. Not much sunlight gets through the canopy at this part of the trail. I noticed the trail was getting wet, soupy and muddy. Up ahead, I saw an imposingly large mud puddle. I picked my line, not my strong suit as a mountain bike rider. I had committed to going around the mud puddle or as much of it as I possibly could. Once again, choosing the wrong line, my front tire struck a big log on the side of the trail, sending me sailing. Dismounting suddenly for my appointment for a mud bath and facial. I had known Peter seven years, but I had never seen him belly laugh like that before. Finding myself chest first into a mud puddle, was like a skit straight out of The Benny Hill Show. I have to admit, it was a classic "Brian" move. Hilarious! Peter and I tried to collect ourselves as we made our way back to where our cars were parked. Through the intermittent chuckles I have to say, there was some serious laughter, going on in those woods. I think Peter found he had as much fun riding a mountain bike out there as I did.

This was the first of many enjoyable rides with friends at Stratham Hill Park with my new-found freedom. Although, there was one Parkinson's symptom I have yet to mention which was very much prevalent in my mountain bike riding. That was fatigue. At the beginning of my bike rides, I felt great, but an hour into the ride I was overcome by fatigue. When this occurs, my response time and decision-making is drastically impaired. Not a good thing when you're out in the woods mountain biking. On one ride with Peter and another good friend Frank, we were about an hour into a ride on a single-track switchback ledge. For no apparent reason at all, I went off-line and ended up on my back down the embankment. Thank god, Peter and Frank were with me. Frank reached down the embankment and hoisted me right out of there like a crane, while Peter went for help. I wasn't hurt at all, though I could have been. This is why I don't ever ride by myself. A flat tire would be a big deal for me to work through on a trail alone. Because I have such trouble walking, being miles in on a ride would spell disaster if my bike failed or if I had an accident. This fatigue issue is a known common problem in Parkinson's patients. When it happens to me on the mountain bike trail, that's when I can make critical mistakes while riding.

Parkinson's disease (PD) feel physically or mentally exhausted? This could be fatigue — a feeling of deep tiredness that does not improve with rest. About half of people with PD report fatigue is a major problem and a third say it is their most disabling symptom.

Fatigue is different from sleepiness. A person who is fatigued feels exhausted, however, does not necessarily feel like sleeping.

Fatigue is common early in the course of PD, but can occur at any point and can happen whether movement symptoms are mild or severe. It is sometimes confused with other symptoms that can make a person sleepy or tired, like sleep disturbances or pain. Fatigue is also a symptom of depression, but a person can be fatigued without being depressed. Stress can make fatigue worse.

No specific cause has been shown to cause fatigue in PD. It is possible that motor symptoms like tremor and stiffness contribute to making muscles tired. But fatigue can have causes outside of Parkinson's, too. It is important to identify and treat illnesses or medications not related to PD that cause fatigue.

The extreme exhaustion that comes with fatigue can lead people to reduce hours at work or retire, or avoid social activities. Understanding fatigue as a symptom of PD and finding ways to cope with it are essential to maintaining a good quality of life. parkinson.org

Tips for Coping with Fatigue
- Eat well.
- Stay hydrated.
- Exercise. Walk, do Tai Chi, dance, cycle, swim, do yoga or chair yoga — whatever you enjoy. Fatigue may make it hard to start exercising, but it may make you feel more energetic afterward. If you find it difficult to get going, consider exercising with another person or a group.
- Keep a regular sleep schedule. If you have difficulty sleeping because of tremor or stiffness, trouble rolling over or needing to use the bathroom, talk to your doctor about these issues.
- Take a short nap (10 to 30 minutes) after lunch. Avoid frequent naps or napping after 3:00 p.m.
- Stay socially connected.
- Pace yourself: plan your day so that you are active at times when you feel most energetic and have a chance to rest when you need to.
- Do something fun: visit with an upbeat friend or pursue a hobby.
- At work, take regular short breaks.

parkinson.org https://www.parkinson.org/Understanding-Parkinsons/
Symptoms/Non-Movement-Symptoms/Fatigue

In my particular case, bringing water, fruit, a few protein bars on bike rides helped keep me from crashing from fatigue and crashing my bike. However, this was by no means a foolproof system. Fatigue was a rather large part of my life with Parkinson's. If I wanted to keep improving as a mountain bike rider, I would need to figure out how to minimize this limitation while riding my mountain bike.

Not long after, I bought the new pedal assist E mountain bike in the spring of 2017, I began having thoughts of participating in the Mount Washington Auto Road Bicycle Hillclimb. This is a bicycle race straight up the Auto Road to the summit of Mount Washington - considered by many pro cyclists to be one of the most challenging hillclimbs anywhere in the world. This thought became a goal and consumed the most driven parts of my being. You're thinking, I must have been nuts,. Right? I would have a difficult time arguing the point with you, but here was my perspective. It had been twenty-five long years since I skied Mont Blanc, and I wanted a physical challenge I wasn't sure if I could do. The feeling of accomplishment upon completing the Vallee Blanche had sustained me and my spirit for such a long time. Now my tank was getting dangerously low, and

I could see another way to replenish my physical spirit. This goal and exercise I took on was to show myself and all the people around me that my spirit is alive and well. Yes, I have Parkinson's disease, but Parkinson's disease will never have my spirit. Not ever!

In late September, early October 2017, I wrote a long email to the event coordinator, Jotham Oliver, of the Mount Washington Auto Road Bicycle Hillclimb. Mr. Oliver works directly for the Tin Mountain Conservation Center which sponsors this race every year. In great detail, I explained to him my physical background and medical history with PD. I stated honestly all of my physical limitations as I saw them at that time, not forgetting to add my recent rediscovery of cycling, through my passion for mountain biking. Reading between the lines, I'm sure what he saw in my email was a novice cyclist requesting to attempt one of the most difficult hillclimbs in the world, and with Parkinson's disease to boot. Oh, I almost forgot. I also requested I would need to ride my pedal assist E mountain bike, Without this critical piece of technology, my attempt to summit would be a physical impossibility. I was pretty sure no rider had ever attempted the MWARBH on a pedal assist E mountain bike like mine before. At least, I didn't think anyone had. Almost right away, I received an honest, caring response back from Mr. Oliver. Jotham told me he would do everything he could do to try to help me with this goal of participating in the 2018 MWARBH. We established a dialog, but he had a few more questions he needed to ask me. He wanted to know what other hillclimbs I had completed. Um, none! Zero! Zip! Nada! Actually, I have never been in a real race in my entire life. He wanted to know a bit more about my health, so I gave him all the information he asked for. He told me he would need to talk to some other folks involved in making a decision, and said, "Hold tight, Brian, and I will get back to you."

Hyper focused, I kept moving towards my goal of participating in the MWARBH race in August 2018. I bought a used indoor exercise bike for training. Wasting no time, I began using this training tool right away, around the same time Mr. Oliver and I started talking about the possibility of my riding in the hillclimb. I trained five days a week on the indoor bike, starting off with small, achievable time goals to build up my wind and stamina. This indoor cycling training was in addition to my Total Gym workouts, which I did five days a week. My training was showing tangible gains, when I got another email from Mr. Oliver. He stated the other people involved in the decision-making had a few suggestions to make. Jotham and these other people believed, having some other hillclimb experience under my belt might be a good idea before I attempted to ride in the Mount

Washington hillclimb. I understood and thought it made good sense. Jotham also said he called the manufacturer of my mountain bike, and they clearly stated to him my bicycle would need multiple batteries to successfully summit the MWARBH. Another valid point I hadn't even considered. By the time in late November I am guessing the answer from Mr. Oliver and the others involved in the decision was not a firm no, but not a yes either. So I took it more like a no to my request to ride in the race. Although Mr. Oliver never said no to me in those terms, but sadly he hadn't given me a green light to participate in this event either.

This news did nothing to slow me down, rather it only seemed to strengthen my resolve. I trained with more intensity, remaining firm on my commitment to make it happen. I told everyone I knew about my goal. In addition, I shared with folks how hard I was training toward it and how committed I was to participate in the event. This made me and my goal real and held me accountable to it. When I ran into friends, they would ask, "Still doing the race, still training Brian?" It helped me with staying on task and remaining focused. I am sure almost everyone thought I was absolutely out of my mind. You see, when the outside world looks at me, they don't expect anything in the way of athletic achievement. In most people's minds, I am dismissed, and castaway to the broken pile. I know differently and expect so much more from myself than that. The human spirit is capable of great achievements if given the opportunity.

I trained through the fall, winter, spring, and into the beginning of the summer. My indoor training bike broke a belt in April. No matter, I was training outdoors on a regular road bike soon after that. I periodically emailed Jotham to check the status or if things had changed. It wasn't until early in July that Mr. Oliver emailed me and said that I was green lighted to be in the race. I could not believe it! He said the only hurdle was acquiring four batteries for my bike, so I would have a chance to finish the race. I told Jotham I would put out my best effort to try to make it happen.

Upon hearing the exciting news from Mr. Oliver, I shared it with my friend Peter. As I mentioned earlier, Peter had an extensive road cycling background. He had participated in the MWARBH twice before and had firsthand experience with what I would be facing. When he heard the news of my approval to ride, he got a little quiet. He didn't seem to be at all enthusiastic about my opportunity to ride in the MWARBH. Not at all! Then Peter told me in his quiet way how he felt. "Brian, I wouldn't do this if I were you." I realized he was coming from a place of love, concern, and friendship for me.

When I asked him why he wouldn't do it, I found some humor in his response. Peter said, "Because you won't ever make it, Brian." My reply was, "That is not my goal, Peter. I just want to have the same opportunity as any other rider to fail or succeed. Stating passionately I just want to participate! I have no delusions of grandeur I am trying to pursue with this goal." At first, I don't think Peter understood where I was coming from. I could tell he was scared for me - the sign of a caring friend. This was about six weeks before the event, and I had no time to be indecisive. Against everyone's better judgment, I listened to my inner voice and called Jotham, committing to the race on August 18, 2018.

Working as a ranger part-time at the golf course takes a physical toll on me during the season. I have a limited supply of energy I am able to draw on. My level of fatigue due to the Parkinson's disease is exacerbated from my work at the golf course. The fatigue is much more apparent to me in season than in the off-season. June, July, and August, the fatigue wouldn't allow me to train on a bike. I just hadn't the energy for it. However, all the training I had done, had been on a "regular bike" forms of training. I purposely left the E bike out of my training regimen. I figured the stronger I got without it, the better I would be when it came time to use the E bike. Through the off-season months on the indoor trainer I was riding fifteen to sixteen miles a day, seventy-five to eighty miles a week. This strategy, I believed, helped me more than I realized. My Total Gym workouts five days a week, continued throughout that time. This kept me gaining strength and flexibility with my body as a whole.

I was growing concerned because all of my efforts to locate four extra batteries for my bicycle were coming up with a big goose egg, and time was running out. I called Jotham to notify him of my dilemma. When I told Mr. Oliver, he said not to worry about it. He would call on a local bicycle shop on my behalf. They should be able to help, he said. Within a few days, he had four extra batteries for my bike. What a relief! This was going to happen!

The other key component I needed to resolve was finding a support driver. Every rider in the race needs to have a support driver to drive them and their bike back down from the summit of Mount Washington. I asked my friend Richard if he wouldn't mind being there to support me with this. Thank god, he said yes. Without Richard, there would be no race for me. As a matter of fact, without Jotham Oliver's efforts, getting me approved, and locating the extra batteries, the event would have never happened for me either.

With Richard now on board, I could relax and focus my attention on the race. Richard is a good and close friend. He always seems to be there for me if ever I need anything. He too, had bought a new mountain bike after I got the pedal assist E mountain bike. Like Peter, he didn't want me to have to ride my bike alone. We have had more than a few unforgettable mountain bike rides together. At the beginning of this adventure, it was Richard who helped me to get the indoor training bicycle to the house. I am so blessed to have supportive friends in my life.

The morning of the race arrived. Richard and I drove to the Mount Washington Auto Road in separate vehicles. We spent the night at Richard's condo in North Conway, New Hampshire. It made much more sense than driving two-and-a-half hours from Hampton, New Hampshire the morning of the race. To say the weather was inclement would be a gross understatement. It poured buckets the entire thirty-minute ride in, from North Conway.

We entered the Auto Road and were directed to parking. I was scrambling to get my bike and myself ready for the start. Nervous, I had butterflies in my stomach, worrying what might lie ahead and my performance. Hearing thunder coming down from up on the mountain, I thought to myself, this can't be good. A few minutes before the start, Mr. Oliver announced there would be a two-hour rain delay, which suited me fine. He said after two hours, we would look at the weather and see if it is clear enough to start the race. Jotham and I met up soon after his announcement. He told me I needed to follow him, and he would introduce me to the people assigned to support me, and my ride. The base of Mount Washington is gigantic. There was no way I could get around such a large of an area walking, so I rode my bike everywhere. As I pedaled behind him, Jotham opened a gate between the Auto Road and the field I happened to be in. I cautiously proceed, following Jotham to a hut on the northern side of the mountain's base. It was there I met four or five nice gentlemen, all HAM radio operators assigned to support my ride. There was one gentleman to my immediate left, tall in stature. He spoke to me, trying to give me some inside information about the race. As I mentioned, I was pretty nervous, mostly because it was all a huge unknown to me. The gentleman began telling me about this particular part of the course, whereas he put it, "All the pro riders wipe out there all the time." He cautioned me to keep an eye out for it. As he spoke of this impending doom, I could feel my colon tighten and anxiety welling up. The man continued on and on about this section of the race. The more he spoke of it, the more my anxiety grew about participating in the race. Finally, I said, "Gentlemen, I need to be getting back." Stressed out of my mind, I put my right foot on my right bike pedal to head back toward the other side of the base. Then, CRASH! I fell with my bike right there. The race hadn't even started, and I was down on the ground. You should have seen the horror in their faces. You could tell what they were thinking. "Oh my god, are we going to have a long day today babysitting this guy." Proudly, I picked myself right up, unembarrassed by the fall and said, "Thank you, gentlemen. I hope to see you up on top," as I rode off toward the south side of the base.

For the next few minutes, I sat in a chair near the event tent, trying to calm down and gather my thoughts. After a while, Jotham announced the race would be starting. Riders, make your way to the starting line. Seeing more than five-hundred world-class athletes gathered at a starting line was quite a dramatic spectacle, I assure you. The announcer called, "First wave!" These are the fastest riders in the race. Then the cannon went off. Boom! I felt my heart leap out of my chest. It was something. I was in the green wave, the last wave of riders. My number was 509, and I actually was the very last rider to cross the starting line for the race.

I was all smiles at the start. However, we would have to see how long that would last. As soon as the race started, my nerves went away, as I began to concentrate on my riding. The first two miles were brutal. Beyond brutal! The steepest grade I had ever ridden a bicycle on by a long shot. When I reached the two-mile mark I was already gassed and out of breath. I remember thinking to myself, what the hell did I sign up for? Are we there yet? Reaching a support car at the two-mile point, I did my first battery change and rested for a bit. The bike battery was not in desperate need of changing, as much as I was in desperate need of resting. After catching my breath, I continued onward. The relentless grade of this mountain road challenged every part of my being, mentally, emotionally, and of course physically. I tried my best to remain steadfast, never waning to the Mount Washington Auto Road's feverish incline.

One thing I found to be helpful was the weather. It was comfortably cool for a mid-August day. Plus the fog was so dense, you were lucky if you could see one-hundred feet in front of you. The fog made it impossible for me to measure my progress as I struggled to ride up to the 7.6 mile summit, which proved to be an advantage. It made me keep my head down and take the course one section at a time.

When I reach the four-mile mark, I felt twice as tired as I had at the two-mile mark. This seemed about right to me, and par for the course. Again, I made a battery change and took a rest. I neglected to mention Jotham had arranged for a support vehicle to follow me up the mountain. Greg, the driver, carried all the extra batteries and stopped every time I needed to stop. He helped me in any way I needed. So I was never completely alone during my ride. It was an altogether safe approach for my ascent up the mountain. Having Greg's support was a huge relief to me.

Somewhere between the fourth mile marker and the fifth mile, I was just about to overtake another racer. As I was passing the gentleman, he said, "Hey, is that as easy as it looks?" I suppose what he really wanted to know was if riding my pedal assist E bike was easy. Out of breath and exhausted, I could not form an intelligent sentence to answer the man. Instead, I just shook my head, no, and kept on riding.

The next few miles were simply a blur. Just more of the same unforgiving, steep incline riding and drudgery. Switchback after switchback. I was hanging in there gaining little by little on the summit. I have to admit, even with the blinding fog, there was a majestic beauty I felt during my ascent up the mountain. The sixth mile mark is where everything changed for me. I could just barely make out my dear friend Richard through the fog, his tall lanky figure standing in the middle of the road. Unbeknownst to me, he had walked down from the summit to cheer on some of the other riders, as well as monitor my progress. This was the first time I had smiled since the start of the race. It wasn't just a smile. I beamed with jubilation. Seeing my friend Richard there, I somehow knew I would finish this challenge. I stopped, while Greg and I made another battery change. Richard asked, "Are you going to do this thing, or what, Brian?" Exhausted, I said, "I'm not quitting yet!" A little more than a mile and a half left to go, I just kept my head down and did what I'd done thus far, which was grind it out. At this point, I really could not feel my legs. They had gone numb with fatigue. Richard walked beside me for a while up the Auto Road. His presence reignited my spirit, and helped me to carry on to the top. Thoughts of my brother came in my head - and other friends and family. I had come so far. I couldn't let them all down, especially myself. In my wildest of dreams, I never thought I would get this far. Now that I had, I really wanted to finish what I had started.

Leaving Richard behind, for the last mile or so it was just me and the mountain. I knew the most challenging part of the ride was still waiting for me at the summit. The final push to the top of Mount Washington, the highest peak in the northeast of the United States had a 22 percent grade - the steepest of the entire journey. I refused to let that fact creep into my thoughts. I figured I would deal with it when I got there.

All of a sudden, I noticed writing on the Auto Road in colored chalk. I saw big hearts with cyclists' numbers in them. I knew the finish line was drawing ever closer. Then out of the fog, I heard muted cheers and cow bells ringing far off into the distance. This was the best sound I had ever heard in my life because I knew the finish was close. I could not see it, but this was the audible alert I needed to start pushing myself, to be able to climb up the 22 percent incline which soon would be facing me. As I took a right-hand turn rounding the last corner, there it was, right in front of me. Moving my weight forward in my saddle to compensate for the extreme grade, I dug in and took an attack position. This was beyond challenging. It pushed me to a level in which I had not been pushed before. This section of the finish was heavily populated with spectators, shockingly, cheering my name. "Go, Brian. Go!" The crowd's cheers spurred me on more and more, digging deeper within myself to make it up the challenging ascent. The cheering, cowbell clanging, and positive energy of the crowd took my focus away from my exhaustion. Then a stranger stepped out from the crowd and came right up to me. As he walked beside me, he gave me words of encouragement. "Come on, Brian, you got this!" "Don't quit!" "Push it!" "Push it!" "Push it!" His encouragement got me to the top of that mountain. As I crossed the finish line, I was greeted with a finishing medal and wrapped in a thick warm blanket. I was so exhausted and depleted from the effort I could not move or dismount my bicycle. My legs had turned to rubber. A number of MWARBH volunteers had to lift me off my bike and place me in a chair. The exact same sense of physical accomplishment and freedom I had felt in 1992, skiing Mont Blanc, was identical to the euphoria I now experienced at the summit of Mount Washington, finishing this hillclimb race. Eventually, Richard made it back to the summit and joined me as I bathed triumphantly in my successful ascent. To say it was a spectacular moment in my life does not paint an accurate or complete picture of this life-changing event. I felt more like I was physically reborn. Reborn in a way I rarely get to feel in my daily life. Finishing the race in two hours, nineteen minutes, thirty-six seconds, I was certainly far off the pace of most of the other riders, but a finish nonetheless. Soon after I crossed the finish line, I learned the identity of the man who helped motivate me, getting me up the last, steep 22 percent grade, which just happened to be the toughest part of the entire hillclimb. His name is Joe Tonon, the MWARBH race finish announcer. Since the finish of the 2018 race, I have been training for the 2019 hillclimb. I am so excited to be participating in this amazing event again.

Chapter 9 - Choose Empowerment

Fear is such a double-edged sword. It keeps us safe and at the very same time holds us back from experiencing some of life's most rewarding opportunities. When my decision-making becomes solely based on my fears, I have learned through the years that I am only short changing-myself. The proudest moments I have had in my life have been when I have pushed myself beyond my fears, regardless of the outcome. Confronting my father, skiing Mont Blanc, and more recently, the Mount Washington Auto Road Bicycle Hillclimb, are just a few moments in which I didn't allow my fear to rob me of a precious opportunity to live. This is the battle we face every day as Parkinson's patients. What we are willing to try to do versus what we are too embarrassed to attempt. At least that has been the true internal struggle throughout my own life. If there is something in your heart to do, I encourage you to follow wherever your heart leads you. Then do it!

I also believe the symptoms of Parkinson's disease are the breadcrumbs to finding out the truth about this disorder. They should be closely studied and researched, not only for a drug therapy solution, but rather a cure. Numbing the symptoms with drugs, in my mind, only delays a potential cure. Drug therapies will never provide a long-term solution to Parkinson's disease. In my case, they have proven to be a short-term pacifier that takes more than it gives back. If NASA went about solving the enormously vast and difficult problems associated with space exploration in the same manner in which we develop cures for diseases, we would never have had a man set foot on the moon.

As I mentioned earlier, how you choose to combat your symptoms today may not work tomorrow. There has been a cost associated with every therapy I have undergone. For instance, the only side effect from the DBS surgery I have experienced has been reduced speech ability and vocal strength. While it is true I can no longer sing, and when I am tired it might be difficult to hear what I am saying, perhaps that is what has helped me find balance. In my life, I feel the benefits have far outweighed this one negative effect of the DBS surgery.

Over time, Parkinson's disease has the ability to erode and rob its victims of every physical human confidence. No matter how your physical symptoms have manifested themselves, eventually we all become conditioned, by our condition, to one degree or another. The art of focusing on what I have and not what I have lost, has continued to serve me well throughout this process. It keeps me on the high side of the daily challenges that I face with the disease and aids in my maintaining a positive mental outlook. This makes swallowing the pill called Parkinson's much more palatable. Regardless, the worry of falling in the late onset Parkinson's patient is frighteningly real. It is a thought with the power to cripple an individual's will to even attempt to leave their home. So, what is the answer? I believe it is the individual's choice to decide what works best for them in their particular situation and try to make self-empowering decisions along the way.

Keeping your spirit alive and well is a full-time job for any of us, not to mention someone who has Parkinson's disease to contend with. Continuing to find new ways to engaged and ignite the physical part of myself, has had enormous benefits in helping me to maintain my spirit in a positive healthy state. It's never easy and by no means, a cake walk, but I have learned that we are all capable of doing much more than we know.

After all, this is not cancer. Parkinson's disease does not abruptly end a person's life. Rather, for most afflicted with the disorder, it impedes profoundly the way you may wish to live your life. The challenge for us, the Parkinson's patient, is finding peace, harmony, balance, and most importantly, acceptance within ourselves, so we can get the most out of the life we have.

I have always maintained a firm belief in the adage, the more you do, the more you can do. I also feel that the opposite holds true. It is my sincerest hope while on your journey with Parkinson's disease, my story has given you some strength, knowledge and empowerment. Thereby providing you with a little relief and optimism, as you experience this wonderful adventure, called life.

Epilogue

As I have aged, I now view my journey with Parkinson's disease as a true blessing that has touched my life. It eventually became a human flaw I could no longer hide from the world, or myself. Hence, the blessing! When I realized that I was unable to ignore the problem away, it forced me to rethink my approach in dealing with this issue. How many of us, myself included, have issues the world can't see? These are the issues that go unaddressed and unresolved possibly forever throughout our lives. We hide them and our insecurities, keeping them secret from everyone, silencing ourselves while stunting our potential. The visibility being afflicted with Parkinson's and its symptoms represents can cause a patient to further retreat inward into seclusion. On the other hand, I began to see and accept Parkinson's disease as the opportunity that it is - the incredible opportunity to meet the most unvarnished version of yourself, while inviting self-acceptance into your own heart. Today, I am finally at peace. I am both grateful and thankful for all I still have in my life and all I still plan and hope to do in the future. I believe no matter where our path takes us, the most crucial ingredient for a healthy life is to do all we can to maintain our spirit. When challenges come, and they will undoubtedly come to everyone, the one thing I have learned I can control, when everything is beyond my control, is my attitude!

Using optimism as a tool to my advantage, my goal every day is to embrace the life I have. The hardships, pain and challenges I face by living simply, and being present I hope to become a better, kinder version of myself today than I was the day before.

For it is in the hardships and pain which life has in store for us where we find a unique part of ourselves. Revealing undiscovered greatness and unforeseen growth. Don't fear it, embrace it.

Resources

Here are just a few of the resources that has continued to provide me inspiration, relief, and helpful information throughout my journey with Parkinson's disease. I hope these resources help you as much as they have helped me to find myself. Good luck!

<u>John Pepper</u>. Meeting John was simply an awe-inspiring eye-opening experience. I am certain that his story will inspire you as much as it did me.
http://www.reverseparkinsons.net

<u>Larry Smith, Ride with Larry documentary</u>. Another inspiring man with Parkinson's disease. This is a must-see film. I watched Ride with Larry just before I started to ride a bike again.
https://www.amazon.com/Ride-Larry-Smith/dp/B01M66UQR4

Parkinson Fit. A website that is dedicated to PD patients that wish to stay active and fit while living with Parkinson's disease. This is an excellent resource for new ideas and motivational stories on how to stay moving in your life with PD.
https://parkinson.fit

Touching the Void. A movie documentary about a true story of Joe Simpson and Simon Yates disastrous and near fatal mountain climb of Siula Grande in the Peruvian Andes, 1985. This adventure and story captures the true nature of the human spirit, refusing to quit. There is also a book by the same title.
https://www.imdb.com/title/tt0379557/

Victoria Arlen. A fellow New Hampshirite, I have found Victoria's story a great source of unbelievable hope and determination in the face of her own medical adversity. If you aren't aware of Victoria's story, it is one that I highly recommend.
https://www.victoriaarlen.com

Rock Steady Boxing. I have never participated in this program; however, it has been a lifesaver for my friend Michael.
https://www.rocksteadyboxing.org

Total Gym. This has been an amazing tool throughout the years. I attribute this machine to my maintaining a successful level of flexibility, and a higher quality of physical health.
https://totalgymdirect.com/?
gclsrc=aw.ds&gclid=EAIaIQobChMI7aqipqHH5QIVDG6GCh3fD
wy1EAAYASAAEgLO6_D_BwE

23andMe and Fox Insight. 23andMe, a genetic research company has teamed up with the Michael J. Fox Foundation recently to aid in the research of PD. The test offered, which is a free test to Parkinson's patients, can tell you if the origin of your particular PD diagnosis was brought on by environmental or genetic reasons. I have attempted to do the PD genetic test with 23andMe twice. Both times my culture came back inconclusive. Sadly, I am not a good reviewer of this service. However, I still think it can be a valuable tool for many other Parkinson's patients.

Fox Insight is a Michael J. Fox Foundation for Parkinson's research online study to gather the world's largest collection of data about life with Parkinson's. 23andMe and The Michael J. Fox Foundation are joining together to launch a sub-study to add genetics to the information collected through Fox Insight.

The goal of the Fox Insight Genetic Sub-study is to accelerate Parkinson's disease (PD) research through a large, longitudinal study combining genetics and patient reported data. Genetic data from the sub-study will be shared broadly to researchers studying PD.

Eligible Fox Insight participants will be invited to participate in the Fox Insight Genetic Sub-study. Learn more about Fox Insight at the following link: https://foxinsight.michaeljfox.org/

Potential participants must be diagnosed with Parkinson's, live in the United States, be 18 years old or older, and complete the first Fox Insight study visit and consent to participate in the Fox Insight Genetic Sub-study. Fox Insight Genetic Sub-study participants who are new to 23andMe will have the option to access the 23andMe Health + Ancestry Service, at no cost. https://www.23andme.com/pd/

The Michael J. Fox Foundation. Arguably the most comprehensive website that I have seen on the subject of Parkinson's disease. https://www.michaeljfox.org

Medtronic. The company I used for my DBS components. Medtronic is a leader in DBS technology.

https://www.medtronic.com/us-en/patients/treatments-therapies/deep-brain-stimulation-parkinsons-disease.html

The Harvard Brain Bank. This facility is the largest brain bank research facility in the country. They offer a host of postmortem brain research services including Parkinson's disease. It is my plan to donate my brain to H.B.B. upon my death.

https://hbtrc.mclean.harvard.edu/about/

Responsible Institute of Technology. Jeffrey Smith is the world's foremost authority on GMOs and chemicals in our food supply. His knowledge and information has helped me so much to eat a cleaner, healthier diet. In addition, Mr. Smith has helped inform me of all the health risks and issues associated with genetically modified organisms in our food.

https://responsibletechnology.org

J.J. Virgin. J.J's approach to diet and food was a key component in my removing sugar and starches from my diet. She armed me with knowledge to maintain a healthier way of life.

https://jjvirgin.com

Davis Phinney Foundation. Davis Phinney is a former professional road bicycle racer from the United States. He was a brazen sprinter and a star of the 7-Eleven Cycling Team in the 1980s and early '90s, and is the leader in race victories by an American, with 328. Another inspirational story of a man never giving up with Parkinson's disease.

https://www.davisphinneyfoundation.org

Parkinson's Disease History. Parkinson's disease has been known to mankind since ancient times. It is referred to in the ancient Indian medical system of Ayurveda under the name Kampavata ("kampa" means tremor in Sanskrit).

In Western medicine it was described by the physician Galen as "shaking palsy" in AD 175. Ancient Chinese sources also provide descriptions that suggest Parkinson's disease.

It was in 1817 that a detailed medical essay was published on the subject by London doctor James Parkinson after whom Parkinson's disease was named. His essay was called "An Essay on the Shaking Palsy." This essay established Parkinson's disease as a recognized medical condition. Parkinson studied and reported six cases in his own practice. (See more.)

https://www.news-medical.net/health/Parkinsons-Disease-History.aspx

Well-Known Individuals With Parkinson's Disease.

Alan Alda - Actor

Michael J. Fox - Actor

George H. Bush - Former U.S. President

Mohammad Ali - Former World Heavyweight
Boxing Champion

Robin Williams - Actor/Comedian

Charles Schultz - Comic Strip Artist

Linda Ronstadt - Musician

Salvador Dali - Artist

Neil Diamond - Musician

Billy Connelly - Actor/Comedian

Billy Graham - Evangelical Christian Leader

Janet Reno - Former U.S. Attorney General

Vincent Price - Actor

Pierre Trudeau - Former Prime Minister of Canada

Roger Banister - World Class Runner

Bob Hoskins - Actor

Kirk Gibson - Pro Baseball Player

Jesse Jackson - Civil Rights Activist

Glenn Tipton - Grammy Winning Guitarist

Dave Jennings - NFL Punter

Leonard Maltin - Movie Reviewer

Ted Kroll - Pro Golfer

<u>Meldrim Thompson Jr.</u> - Former Governor of New Hampshire

<u>Terry Thomas</u> - Actor/Comedian

<u>Pat Torpey</u> - Musician

<u>John Paul II</u> - Pope

<u>Adolf Hitler</u> - Chancellor of Germany

<u>Parkinson's Foundation Notable People.</u>
https://parkinson.org/Understanding-Parkinsons/Statistics/
Notable-Figures-with-Parkinsons?
gclid=EAIaIQobChMIx5ejzqCJ4QIV08DICh30XwGpEAAYAiAAE
gL72fD_BwE

<u>People That Thrive In The Face Of Medical Adversity.</u>
https://medium.com/thrive-global/how-to-keep-going-in-the-
face-of-adversity-f60861b8170b

https://www.health.com/health/article/0,,20411525,00.html

<u>Famous People With Numerous Diseases & Challenges .</u>
https://www.thefamouspeople.com/disease-disability-list.php

<u>Multiple Sclerosis.</u>
https://www.everydayhealth.com/hs/multiple-sclerosis-pictures/
seven-athletes-with-ms-who-kick-butt/

<u>Cerebral Palsy.</u>
https://www.everydayhealth.com/healthy-living-pictures/seven-
famous-people-with-cerebral-palsy.aspx

Amputees.
https://www.ranker.com/list/famous-amputees/celebrity-lists

Bethany Hamilton. One of my favorite stories in human perseverance ever. Bethany lost her left arm to a shark attack as a young girl. Within a few years, her dream of becoming a pro surfer was realized.
https://bethanyhamilton.com

You are not alone. The loss which you are feeling is extremely real and is shared by just about every human being on our planet, in one form or another. Wherever you can find inspiration, let it lift you and your spirit upward towards a happier and more productive life. Inside each one of us is the power and strength to take back our lives. You just need to want it bad enough to keep on going.

A Final Word

I firmly believe that as time goes on more and more foreign chemicals, herbicides, pesticides, pollutants and carcinogens will enter our air, oceans, rivers, drinking water, land, soil, crops and of course our food supply. As these foreign materials increase, so too, will the numbers of cases of not only Parkinson's disease, but many other diseases and neurological disorders as well. I urge us all to try to do our parts to protect our planet, and ourselves from a fate such as this. Each one of us has the power to make a difference. As I have heard Michael J. Fox say on so many occasions pertaining to Parkinson's disease, "Genetics loads the gun, and the environment pulls the trigger."

The herbicide, "Paraquat," has been scientifically linked as a cause of Parkinson's disease.

Paraquat (trivial name; /ˈpærəkwɒt/) or *N,N'*-dimethyl-4,4'-bipyridinium dichloride (systematic name) is an organic compound with the chemical formula $[(C_6H_7N)_2]Cl_2$. It is classified as a viologen, a family of redox-active heterocycles of similar structure. Paraquat was manufactured by Chevron. This salt is one of the most widely used herbicides. It is quick-acting and non-selective, killing green plant tissue on contact. It is also toxic to human beings and animals due to its redox activity, which produces superoxide anions. It has been linked to the development of Parkinson's disease[5][6] and is banned in several countries.

Paraquat may be in the form of salt with chloride or other anions; quantities of the substance are sometimes expressed by cation mass alone (paraquat cation, paraquat ion).

The name is derived from the *para* positions of the *quaternary* nitrogens.

wikipedia.org https://en.wikipedia.org/wiki/Paraquat

https://parkinsonsnewstoday.com/2017/10/27/technique-explains-herbicide-link-parkinsons-disease/

For many years there has been discussions in the Parkinson's research community about, "Free Radicals," and the role that they may or may not play in Parkinson's disease. Here is some additional information for you to research and look into.

Free Radicals in Parkinson's disease. Although there are a number of hypotheses to explain the pathobiochemistry of Parkinson's disease (PD), the one on oxidative stress (OS) has gained major interest. The evidence for OS participation as a cause of PD can be summarized as follows: 1) OS is involved in physiological aging, 2) there is ample evidence that OS is significantly enhanced in PD compared to age-matched healthy persons, 3) OS is an early feature of PD because OS-dependent aggregation of proteins in the form of advanced glycation end products can be imaged in Lewy bodies at a time in a person's life, when no phenotype of a neurodegenerative

disorder is evident, 4) Experimental models of PD show OS and degeneration of dopaminergic neurons. The toxin-induced neurodegeneration can be blocked by antioxidants, and 5) Activated microglia, known to release free radicals and inflammatory cytokines, are present in brains of Parkinsonian patients. In conclusion, a great body of evidence points to the view that OS is a major component underlying the pathobiochemistry of PD. Together a genetic disposition and endogenous/exogenous toxic events of various origins result in a synergistic cascade of toxicity which leads to dysfunction and finally to cell death of dopaminergic neurons. Again, OS plays a significant role in generating cell death signals including apoptosis.
pubmed.gov https://www.ncbi.nlm.nih.gov/pubmed/12375056

It might surprise you to learn that free radicals can be caused by the drug therapies prescribed for Parkinson's disease.

Does levodopa accelerate Parkinson's disease?
Therapeutic options for the treatment of Parkinson's disease (PD) have expanded tremendously over the last 5 years, although levodopa remains the gold standard of therapy. A major therapeutic controversy has been the question of levodopa's potential to cause toxic effects on nigrostriatal cells, thus potentiating the progression of the disease. The answer to that question will guide physicians in the timing of levodopa initiation and its dosage. The issue of levodopa toxicity was initially raised because of its potential to cause long term adverse effects (dyskinesias and motor fluctuations), which are not observed in untreated patients. Levodopa-induced toxicity can be related to its potential to produce free radicals, which are known to be toxic to cells, in the process of its conversion to dopamine. In vitro data reveals some evidence of the toxic effect of levodopa although recent studies suggest that levodopa toxicity is dependent on its concentration and can be ameliorated in the presence of glial cells. In vivo data from healthy animals and humans does not convincingly demonstrate levodopa toxicity. There is no evidence of levodopa-induced neurotoxicity in patients with PD. Despite the absence of toxic effect in patients with PD, levodopa can cause long term complications like motor fluctuations and dyskinesias and should be used judiciously in the minimal clinically effective dose. In this article we review evidence for and against levodopa neurotoxicity and the implications of the 'levo-dopa controversy' on clinical practice.

pubmed.gov https://www.ncbi.nlm.nih.gov/pubmed/10408739

Free Radical Toxicity and Antioxidant Medications in Parkinson's disease.
https://academic.oup.com/ptj/article-pdf/78/3/313/10762024/ptj0313.pdf

With all the potentially damaging properties in our environment and contained in our food supply these days, making good choices and decisions is seemingly getting more and more challenging for everyone. Besides having Parkinson's disease itself to deal with, negotiating the potential pitfalls of prolonged use of a drug therapy program to combat symptoms, finding a healthy balance that works for you can be illusive. Never ever give up on yourself or your quest to be healthier. While managing your disorder can be a never-ending barrage of exhausting hard fought decisions, we never know what might be right around the corner that may offer relief to our medical situation.

A Special Thanks

To Jotham Oliver with the Tin Mountain Conservation Center and Lisa Mathews McCoy, from the Mount Washington Auto Road. Your support helped me make my dream of riding my bicycle to the summit of Mount Washington come true. Thank you so much, Jotham and Lisa. I consider you both good friends.

~ Family Scrapbook ~

Me   **Mark**

Mom

Dad   Mark   Mom

Mom & Dad

Mark

Mark **Mom** **Me**

Me & Mark wedding

Dad & Mom

Mark & his 442

Me at work

Me 80's

Me performing 90's

Me 2013

Mark

Me playing tennis 80's

2003-2005

Overweight, on meds - Pre - DBS

2013-2015

In balance, off meds - Post - DBS

After the 2018 MWARBH Race.

PHOTO BY: IOANNA RAFTIS / EDIT BY: BRIAN HALL

BRIAN HALL
LET'S TAKE THE PARK OUT OF PARKINSON'S

Join the Movement!

Self-Published by, Brian Hall

Through

Website: https://notafraidtofall.com

Available on the BookBaby Book-Shop website

and most other major book retailers.